GAINSBOROUGH'S COTTAGE DOORS

An Insight into the Artist's Last Decade

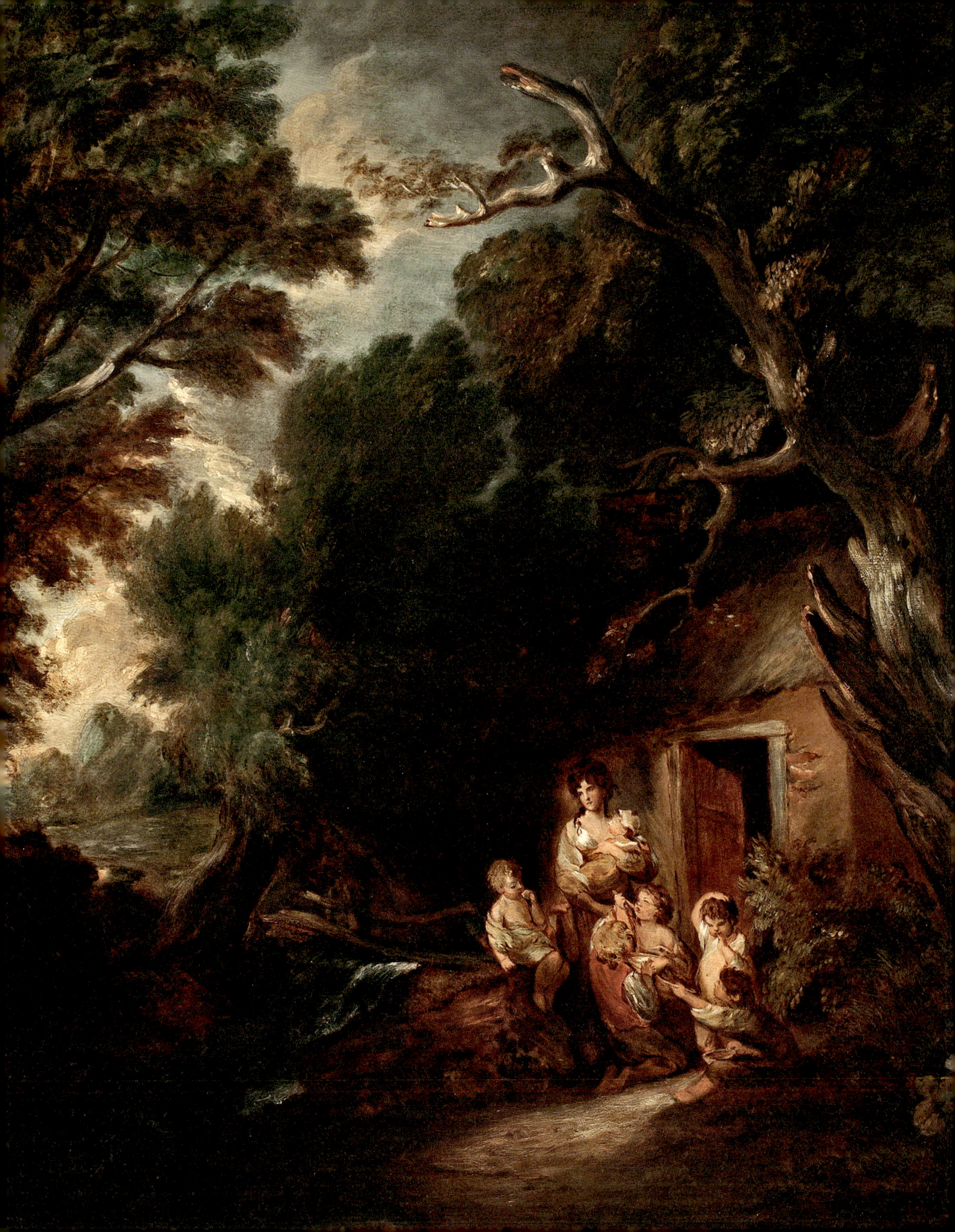

GAINSBOROUGH'S COTTAGE DOORS

An Insight into the Artist's Last Decade

Hugh Belsey

Paul Holberton publishing

COPYRIGHT

This book is published to accompany the exhibition
*Revisiting the Cottage Door: Gainsborough's Masterpiece
in Focus* at The Huntington Library, Art Collections, and
Botanical Gardens, San Marino, California, from 1 June
to 2 December 2013.

© 2013 the author

ISBN 978 1 907372 50 6

British Library Cataloguing in Publication Data
A catalogue record for this book is available from the British Library

Produced by Paul Holberton publishing,
89 Borough High Street, London SE1 1NL
www.paul-holberton.net

Designed by Laura Parker
www.parkerinc.co.uk

Origination and printing by E-Graphic, Verona, Italy

FRONT COVER, FRONTISPIECE: Detail of Stunt *Cottage Door* (cat. 2)
BACK COVER: Thomas Gainsborough, *Wooded landscape, c.* 1775 (fig. 41)

CONTENTS

FOREWORD

Since it was first opened to the public in 1928, the Huntington
Library, Art Collections, and Botanical Gardens in San Marino, California,
has been associated with the work of Thomas Gainsborough. Its collections
contain some of his greatest masterpieces, including the celebrated 'Blue
Boy', the famous portrait of the musician Carl Friedrich Abel, and one of
the artist's finest landscapes, *The Cottage Door*, painted in 1780. In 2005,
The Huntington collaborated with the Yale Center for British Art on an
exhibition exploring Gainsborough's varied treatment of the theme of the
Cottage Door (*Sensation and Sensibility: Viewing Gainsborough's 'Cottage Door'*),
placing the work within the social, cultural and scientific contexts of late
eighteenth- and early nineteenth-century Britain. Since then, however, two
autograph versions of *The Cottage Door* have surfaced.

This volume is published in conjunction with a focused installation
at The Huntington that brings together, for the first time, these three
versions of *The Cottage Door*. It is our hope that this close examination
of a great painting rendered in triplicate – with subtle but important
differences between each version – will encourage viewers to take another
look at a masterpiece we thought we knew. The project to re-examine our
understanding of *The Cottage Door* was the inspiration of Hugh Belsey,
whose intimate knowledge of Gainsborough's painting technique and studio
practice are second to none. At The Huntington, thanks for overseeing the
exhibition are particularly due to Catherine Hess, Chief Curator of European
Art, and Melinda McCurdy, Associate Curator of British Art, with additional
thanks owed to Jacqueline Dugas, Susan Colletta, Gregg Bayne, Tom Cabell,
Brian Mains and Christian Mounger.

James Stunt, owner of one of the newly surfaced paintings, first proposed
the display of the three versions of *The Cottage Door* at The Huntington. He
has generously met the expenses of the exhibition and the production of the
publication, as well as kindly lending us his painting, for which we are deeply
grateful. We are also indebted to the third owner, who graciously agreed to
lend us his version, as well as to Maxwell Anderson, Eugene McDermott
Director of the Dallas Museum of Art, where the painting is on loan, for his
willingness to part with it for the duration of our exhibition.

Kevin Salatino
Director

Detail of the Huntington *Cottage Door* (cat. 1)

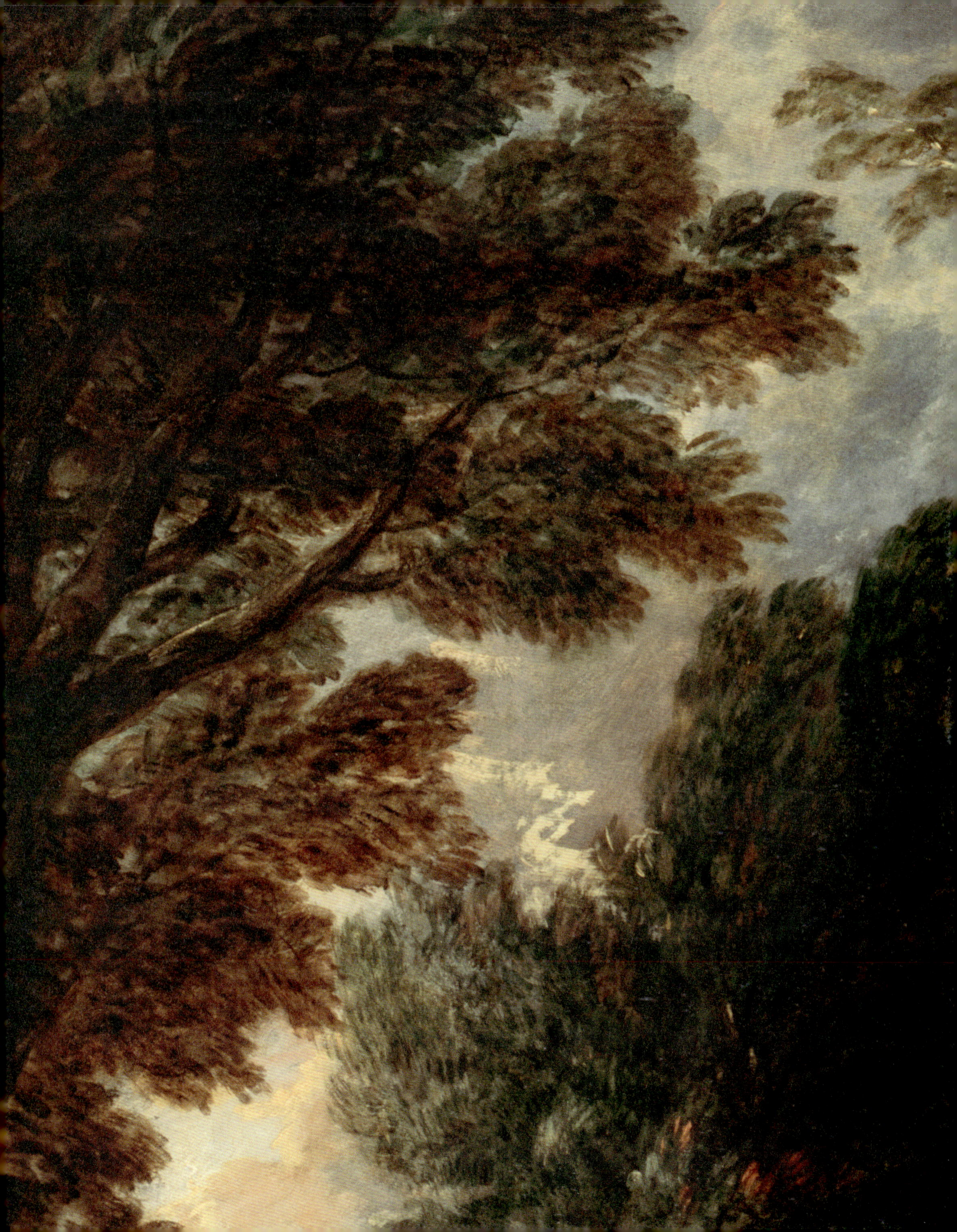

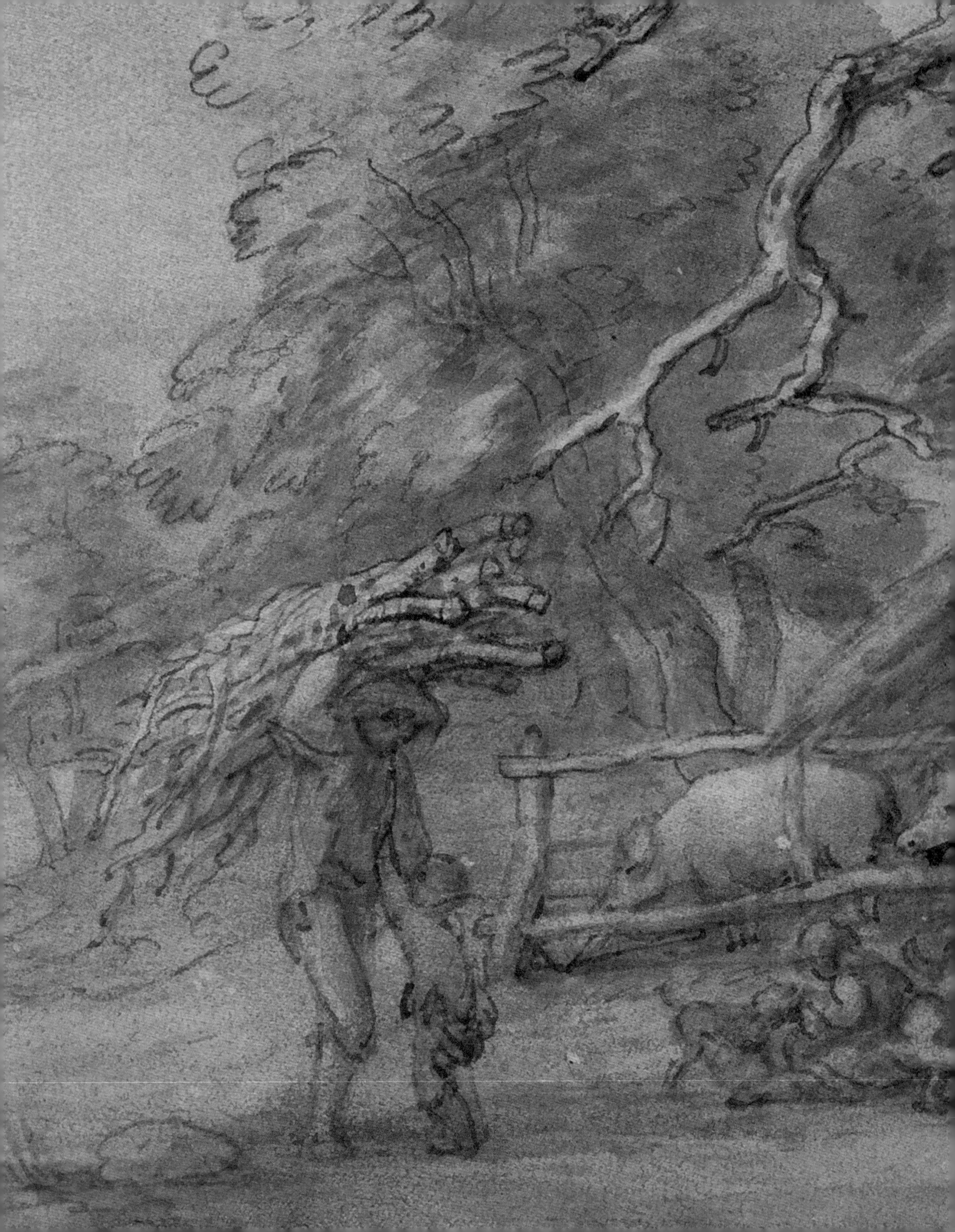

ACKNOWLEDGEMENTS

THIS PROJECT HAS GROWN FROM A MONTH-LONG FELLOWSHIP
at The Huntington in June 2012 and I am delighted that my time there has
borne such lasting fruit. Without the acceptance, generosity, openness and
kindness of so many of the staff this project would have died in the bud.
I should like especially to thank the members of the art department, Kevin
Salatino, Catherine Hess, Melinda McCurdy, the department registrar,
and Jacqueline Dugas, for responding to the idea with such alacrity and for
ensuring that the display shows such characteristic panache. Without the
infectious enthusiasm of James Stunt this project would never have come
about and I am most grateful to him. Paul Holberton readily accepted
the challenge of producing the accompanying book and, with their usual
precision, he and Laura Parker have produced an elegant book that lives up
to Gainsborough's artistic distinction.

Others have helped me too. I am most grateful to Philip Mould
of Historical Portraits Ltd, who reappraised both the other versions of
The Huntington *Cottage Door* and who has provided much of the research
material for this book. While I was writing this essay studies were also being
undertaken on the Daubuz copy and its owner very kindly met my travel
expenses in order for me to study the painting in New York. My thanks,
too, to Caroline Oliphant of Bonhams, Lowell Libson, Simon Gillespie and
Deborah Gage, who have shown me works of art that feature in this book.
Finally, I am indebted to Susan Sloman, who kindly read the manuscript and
corrected errors that had slipped the attention of the author; her generosity
has made this a better book. I thank them all.

Hugh Belsey
Bury St Edmunds
May 2013

Detail of *Wooded landscape* (fig. 41)

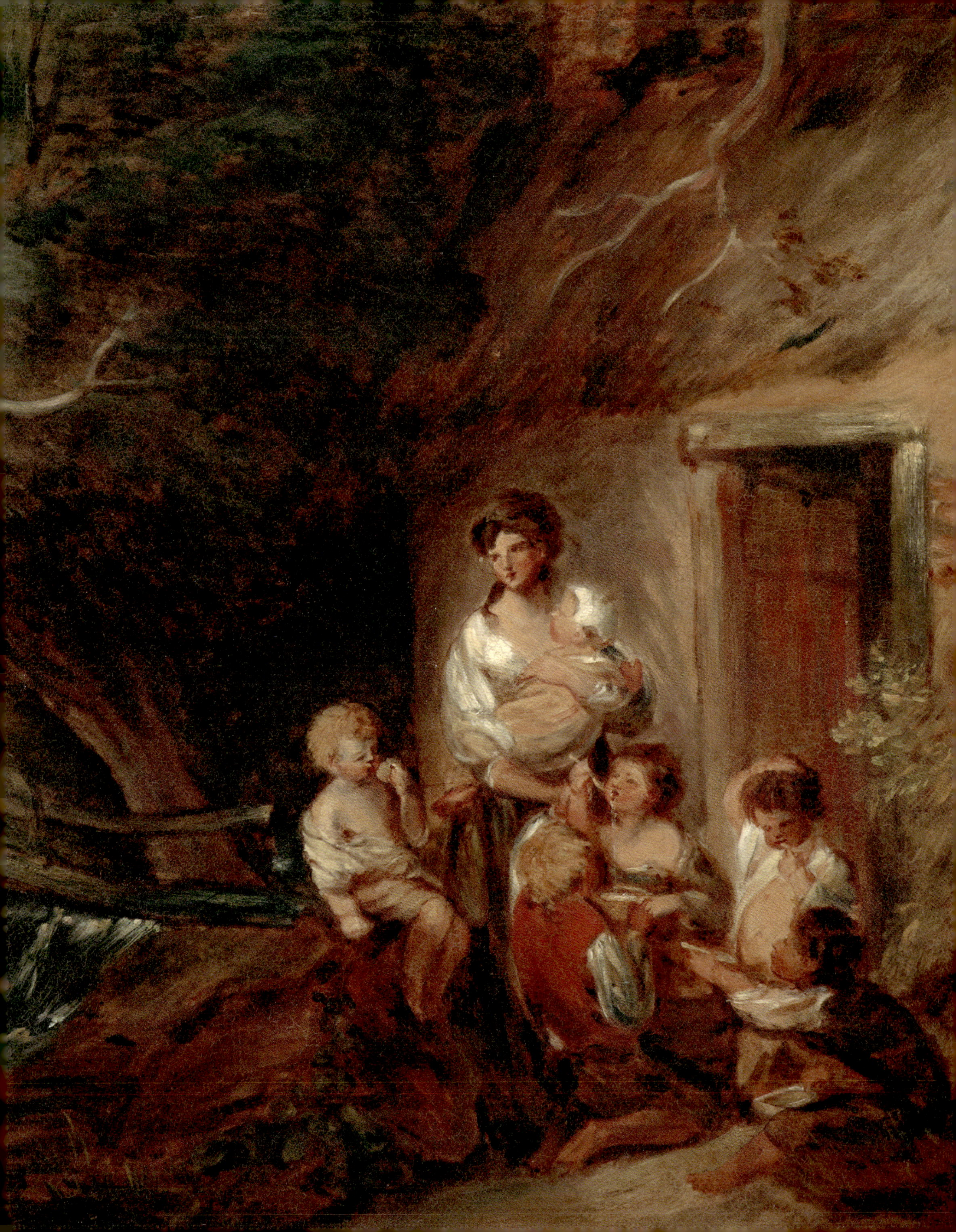

A Background of Dissent

THE WORK OF THOMAS GAINSBOROUGH (1727–1788) is characterized by a series of subjects that preoccupied him, which with time he was able to hone and define more clearly. These themes have been masked by his work as a portraitist, in which the client necessarily dictated – and, of course, generally was – the subject (though the composition of the canvas was the painter's invention). But in his landscape paintings, his so-called 'fancy pictures', and his copies after Old Masters, Gainsborough shows a predisposition to stick with an idea, revisit it, review it and reprise it over many years.

In 2005, for an exhibition at the Yale Center for British Art, New Haven, and The Huntington Library, San Marino, Ann Bermingham made an exhaustive study of the 'cottage door' theme and, more recently, Susan Sloman has investigated the artist's recurrent ideas in his landscape paintings in her recent exhibition *Gainsborough's Landscapes: Themes and Variations* at the Holburne Museum of Art in Bath.[1] Bermingham's book centred on the painting exhibited at the Royal Academy in 1780 that is now in The Huntington Art Collections in California (cat. 1). Including, without discussion, a reproduction of one of the two recently discovered versions of this work that feature in the current display, it investigated the iconography of the subject and the context in which its early owners displayed the Huntington picture. The appearance of these other two versions (cat. 2 and 3), however, reveals an aspect of Gainsborough's work that is more searching and therefore prompts further investigation into the repetitive nature of the artist's work. A study of his unconventional background, training and early development as an artist provide some clues as to why Gainsborough used painting in this very personal way.

*Gainsborough's
Cottage Doors*

Gainsborough was essentially self-taught. According to tradition he learned to draw in the fields and meadows around his birthplace, Sudbury in Suffolk, playing truant and forging notes from his father to excuse himself from school. His family, whose main trade was dealing in bays and says – fine worsted cloths – were Dissenters. All of this must have contributed to the independence of attitude and mind that was to shape his future. In about 1740 he moved to London, where a short apprenticeship with a silversmith – just like the training of William Hogarth – gave him the rudiments of engraving and sharpened his eye to the use and subtlety of line. He learned more about drawing, however, at the St Martin's Lane Academy, often by osmosis, through the teaching of the Frenchman François Hubert Gravelot and by rubbing shoulders with gifted fellow pupils.

Francis Hayman had been commissioned to paint 53 large-scale paintings to decorate the supper-boxes at Vauxhall Gardens, which were completed in 1741/42. There is evidence that, with many others, Gainsborough helped with their production, and this would have aided his technical understanding of painting in oils. He would certainly have seen the work of Hogarth and, though it is not known whether the young artist was mentored by him, he must have used Hogarth's crisp and exacting technique (fig. 1) as a benchmark for his own work. Recognition came in 1748, when he was chosen, along with his contemporaries Samuel Wale, Richard Wilson and Edward Haytley, to paint views of London hospitals to decorate the Courtroom of the Foundling Hospital, a commission which appears to have been masterminded by Hogarth. By the end of the 1740s Gainsborough was regarded as something of a landscape specialist, contributing background views to portraits by Hayman (fig. 2). The lessons learned from Hayman and Hogarth served him well and he was

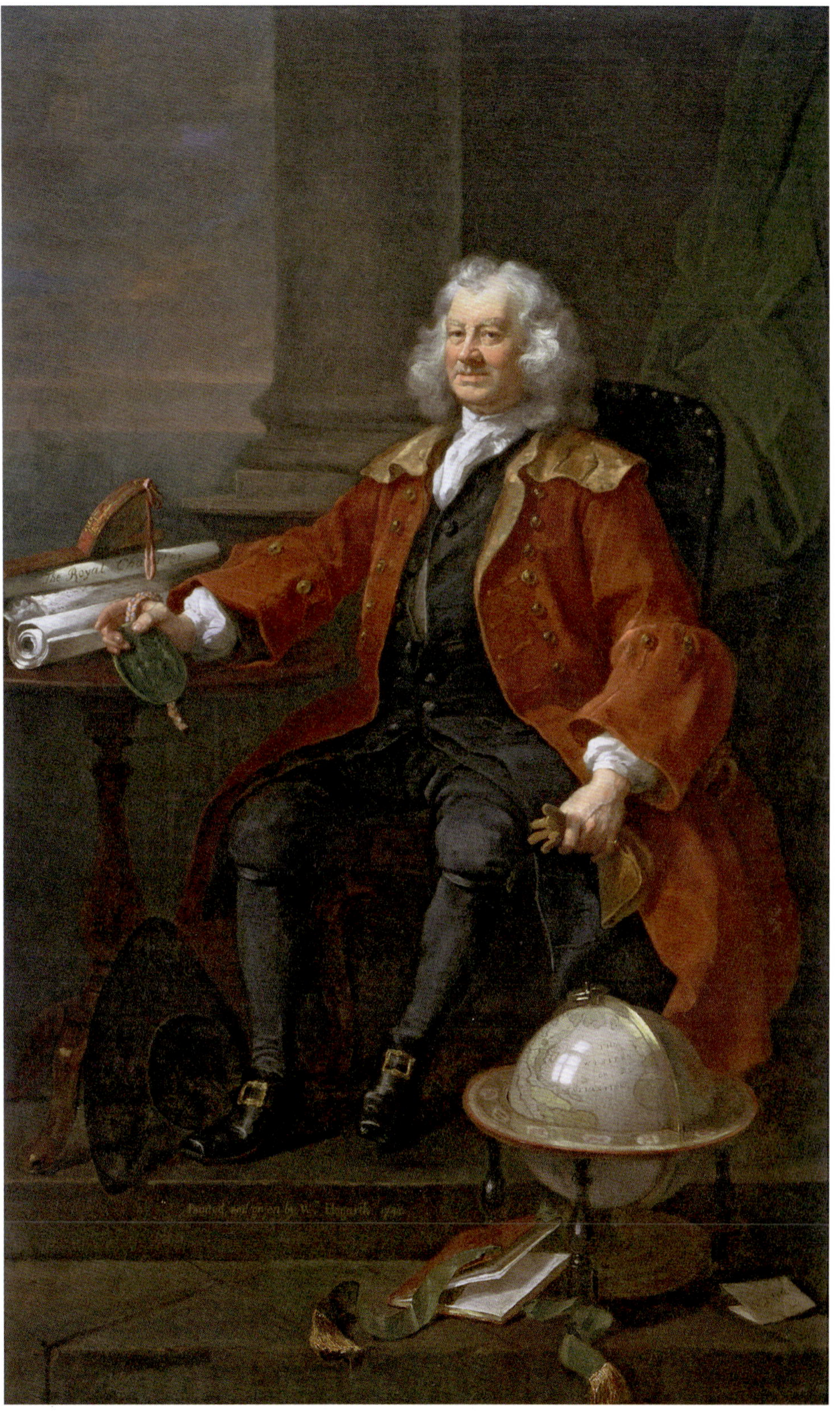

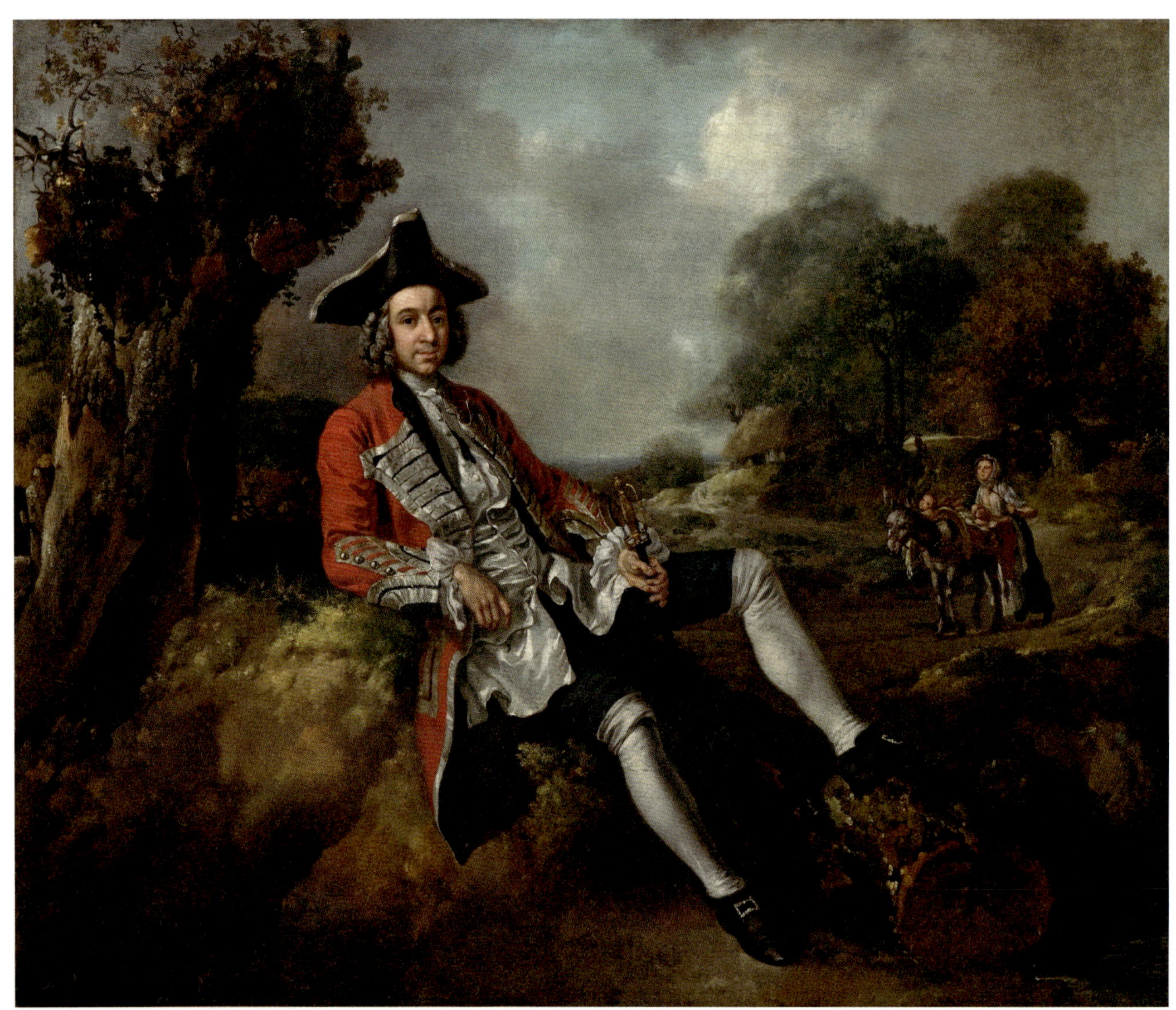

Detail of fig. 2

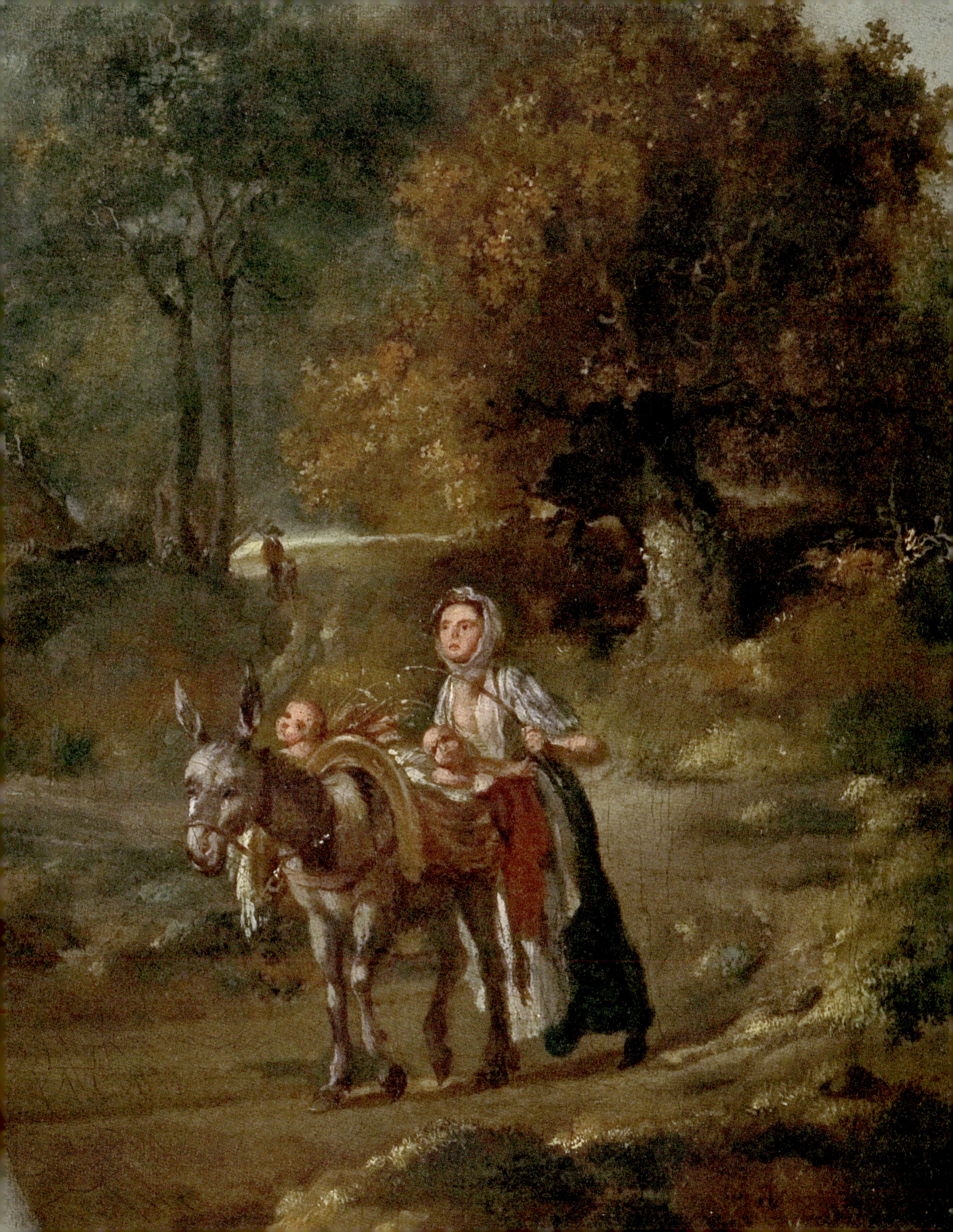

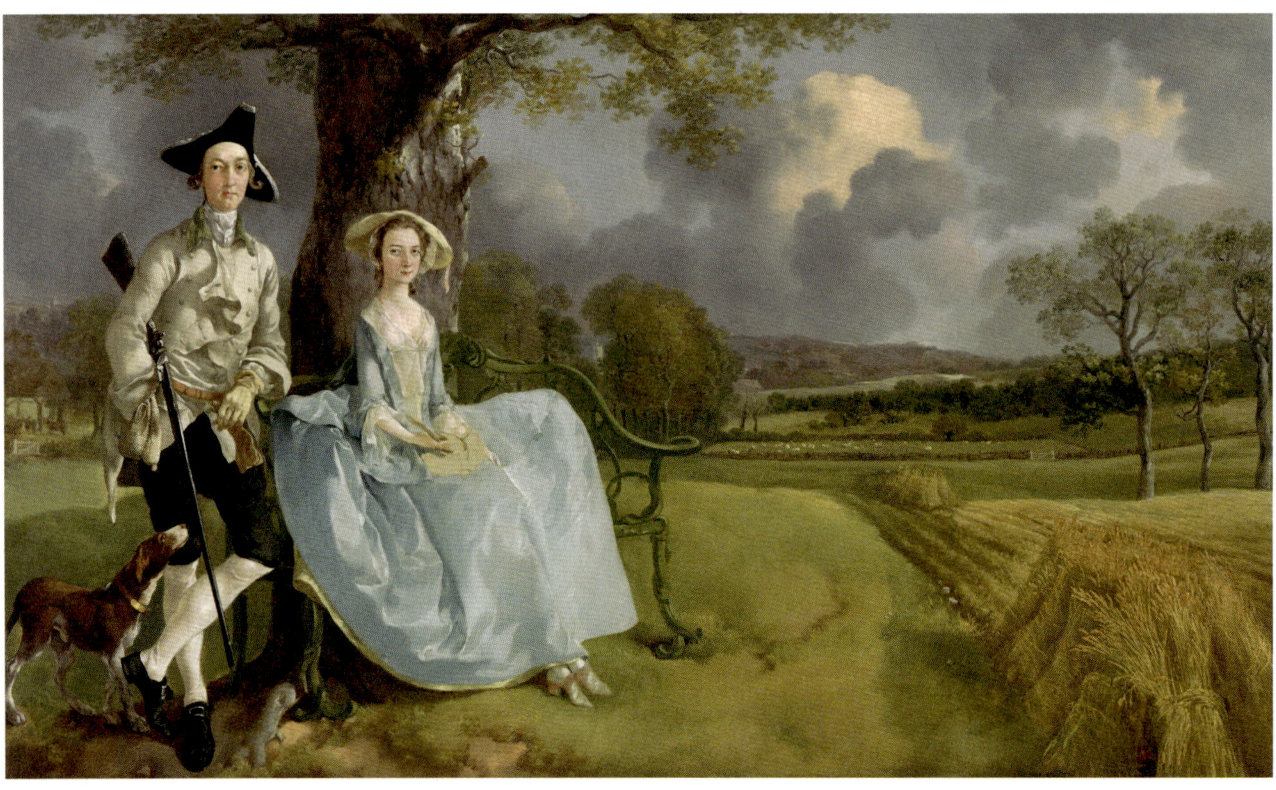

*Gainsborough's
Cottage Doors*

evidently considered to have an affinity for painting in oils: his old teacher, Gravelot, used him to paint figure subjects from his designs.[2]

Family responsibilities encouraged his return to Suffolk, and it was there that he was able to assimilate the hard lessons he had learned in London and to begin to produce portraits in landscapes that unify sitters and landscape with a unique integrity, as shown in the justly famous portrait of Mr and Mrs Andrews (fig. 3). In the late 1750s, conscious that the market for portraiture had shifted, he changed direction and learned to catch a likeness by painting a series of straightforward head-and-shoulder portraits

Detail of fig. 3

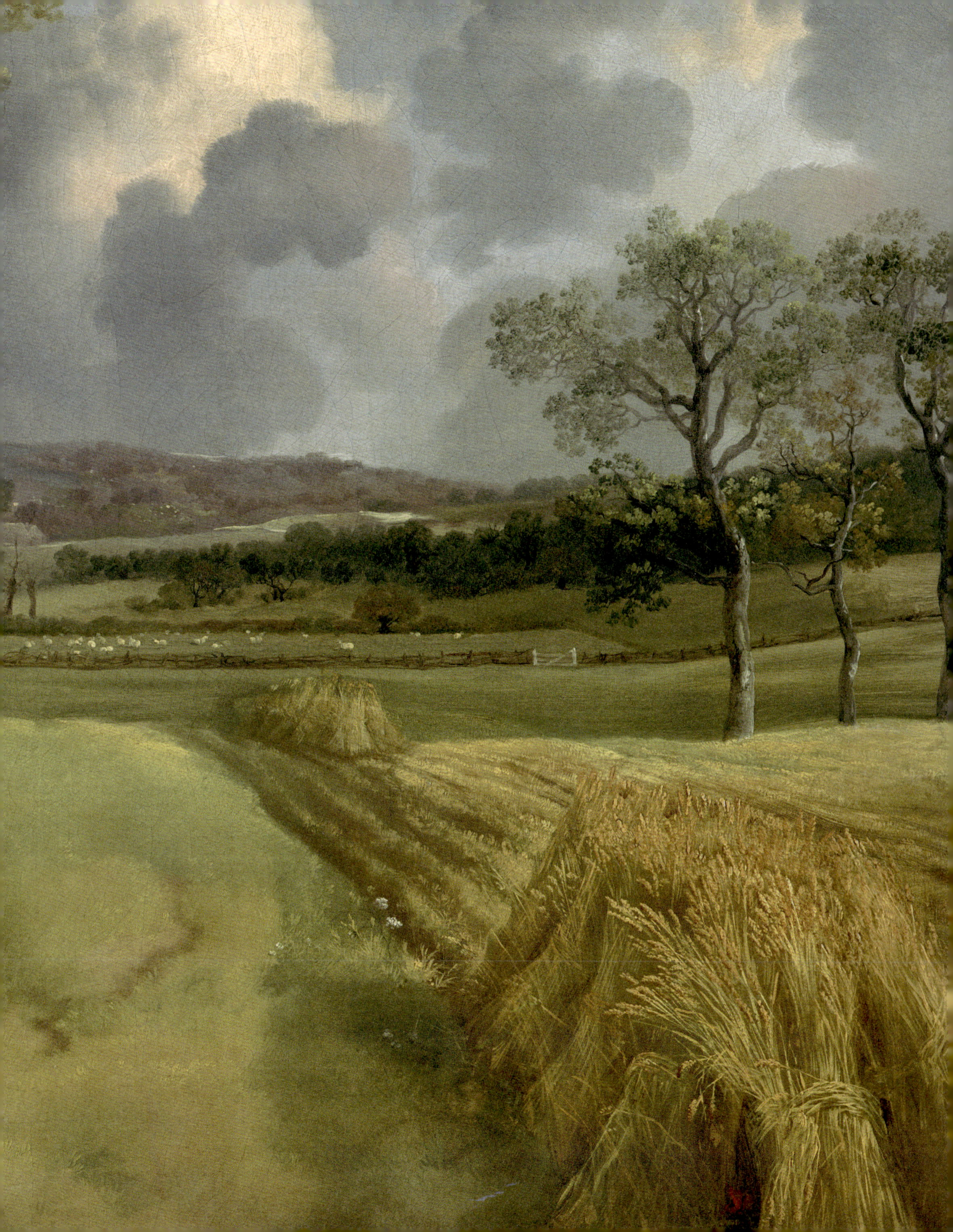

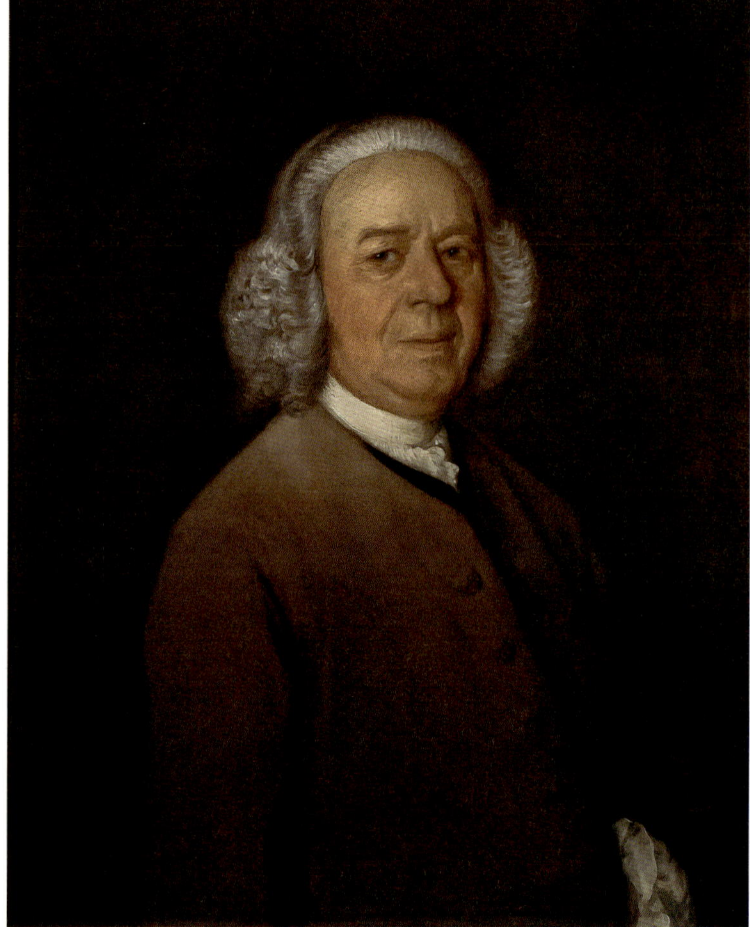

(fig. 4). Haphazard though this training had been, he then felt able to meet the challenges of moving to Bath, where there was a much livelier social scene, more visitors and the opportunity of more portrait commissions.

After a six-month stay in Bath that started in the autumn of 1758, he decided that moving to the city would be worthwhile and returned to Ipswich to sell up and take his family to the West Country. His art at the time was developing at such a rate that after just a couple of years in Bath his work was as immediate and responsive as that of any other painter working in Britain. But such an individualistic beginning, without the cosseting of an artist's studio, and such independence of thought, made him suspicious of any organization governed by rubric. He would have been glad, however, of the creation, soon after his arrival

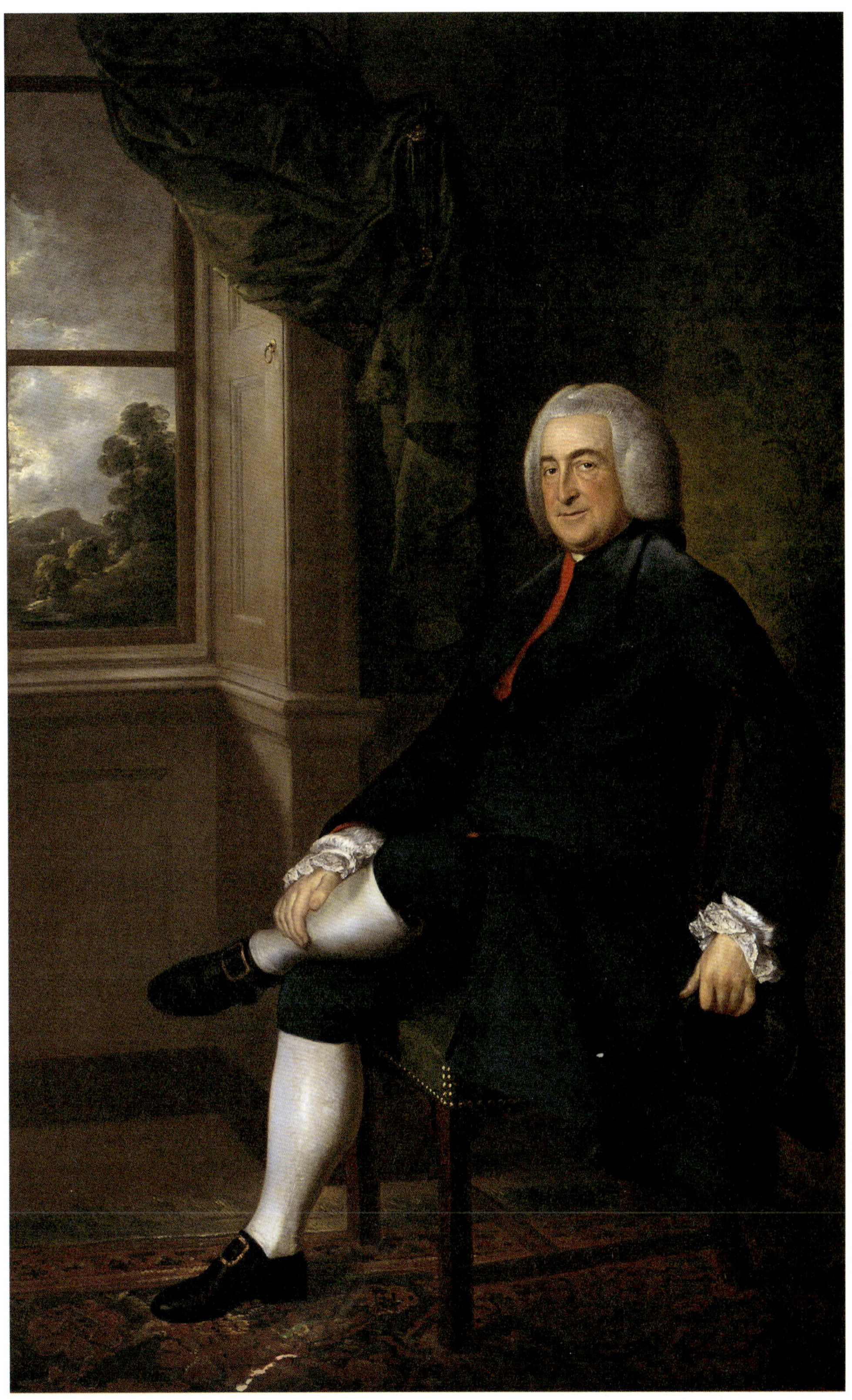

FIG. 6
Thomas Gainsborough
Joshua Kirby and his wife, Sarah,
c. 1747 and *c.* 1753
Oil on canvas 74.3 × 61.6 cm
National Portrait Gallery, London

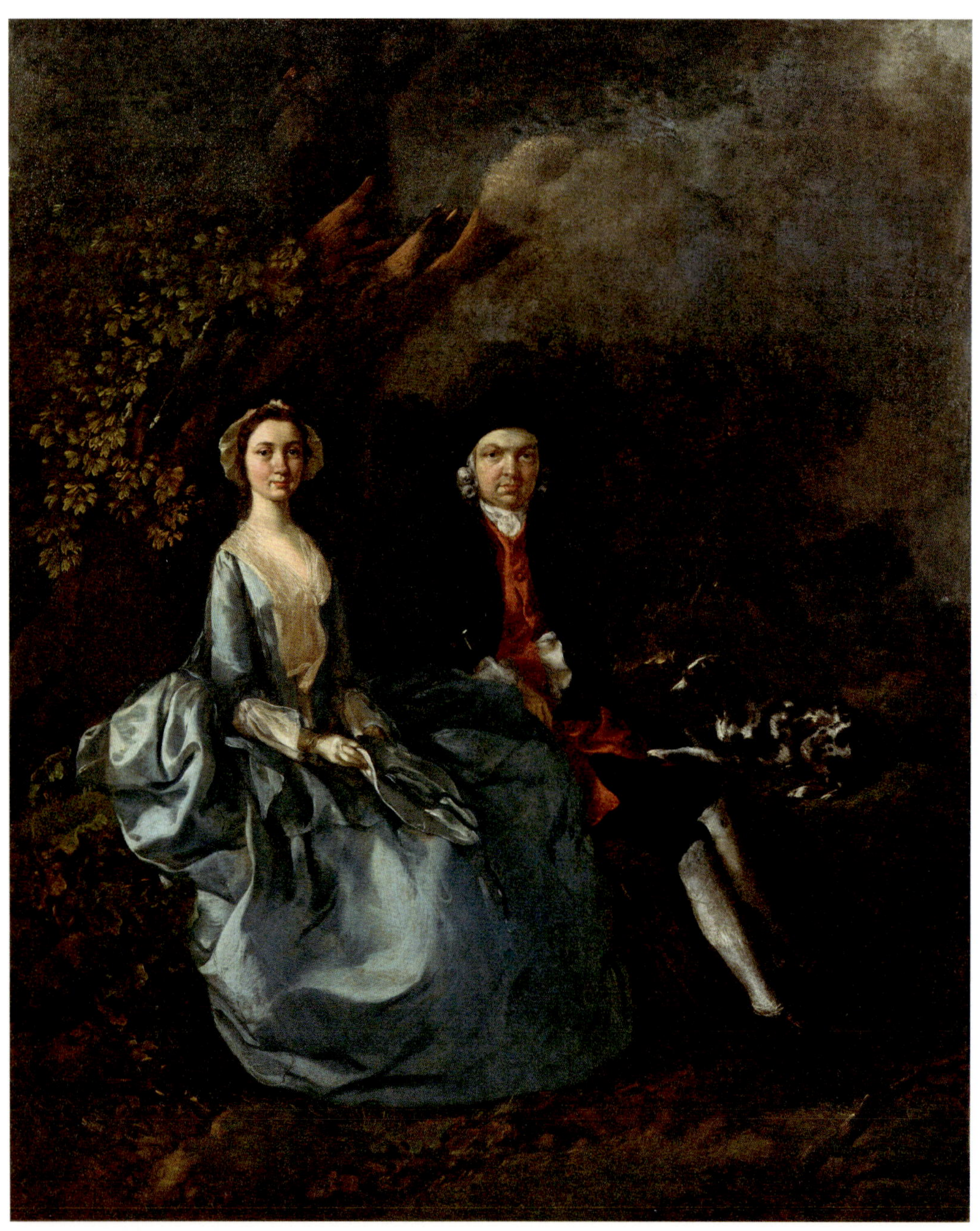

in Bath, of the Society of Artists, formed to support artists and
their families who had fallen on hard times. Its main activity was
to form an annual exhibition of works by different artists so that
visitors could compare and contrast the relative merits of each
exhibitor. Gainsborough contributed to the exhibitions, each
year submitting the most innovative works he had created in the
previous twelve months (fig. 5). He must have felt gratified by
the appointment in 1768 of his long-standing Suffolk friend and
collaborator Joshua Kirby as President of the society. It would have
given him a closer association with the organization.

Joshua's father John Kirby was a well-known figure in Suffolk,
having surveyed the county and published his findings in *The
Suffolk Traveller* in 1735. Gainsborough painted Kirby and his wife
Sarah (fig. 6) and collaborated with Joshua in a painting of the
church of St Mary's, Hadleigh, in about 1748 (private collection,
on loan to Gainsborough's House, Sudbury). Although ten years
his senior, Joshua must have been amongst the artist's closest
friends: Gainsborough painted him in an unfinished portrait
(Victoria and Albert Museum, London) and in a lacklustre head-
and-shoulders portrait (Fitzwilliam Museum, Cambridge). Joshua
Kirby's own reputation was founded on the publication in 1754 of
*Dr Brook Taylor's Method of Perspective Made Easy, both in Theory and
Practice,* to which Hogarth contributed a humorous frontispiece. It
served him well, and in 1756 Kirby moved from Suffolk to London
to teach the Prince of Wales perspective, then, after the accession
of George III in 1760, he tutored the royal children. Shortly after
Kirby became President of the Incorporated Society of Artists
(it had been renamed in 1765), a coup marginalized both him and
the society, and resulted in the founding of the Royal Academy.

Gainsborough must have regarded the foundation of the
Academy with grave misgivings. The negotiations had ostracized

Tombs of Joshua Kirby (foreground)
and Thomas Gainsborough (background),
St Anne's churchyard, Kew

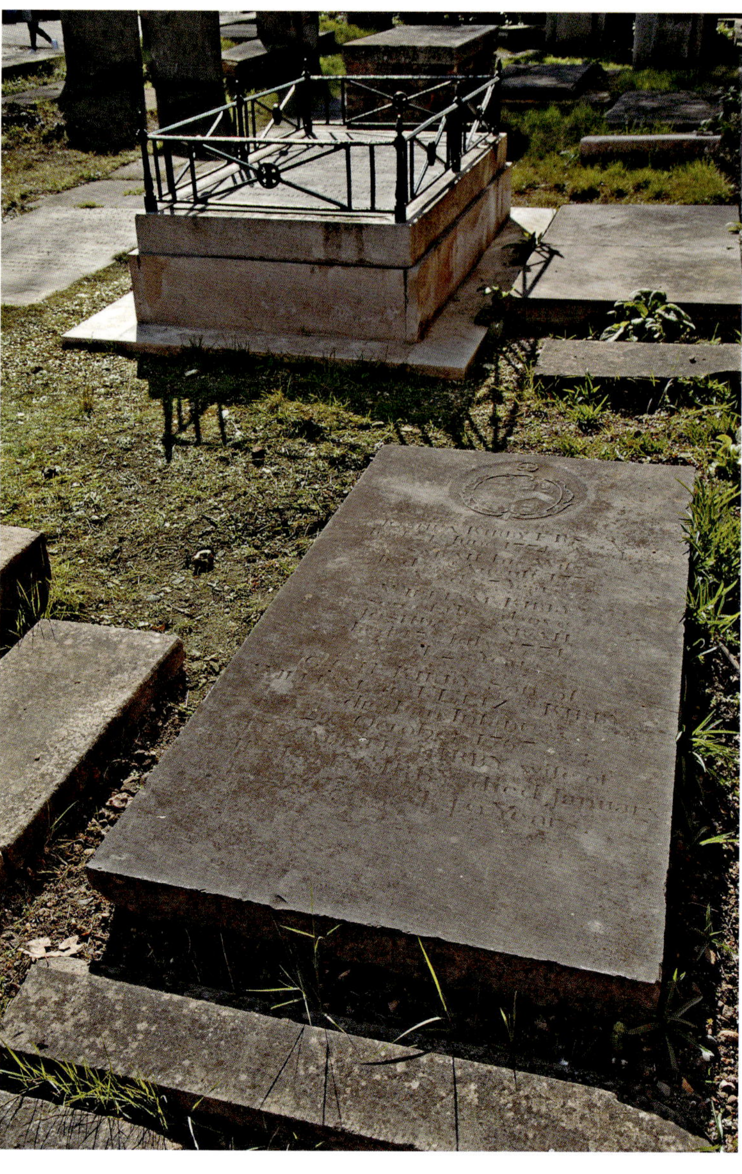

*Gainsborough's
Cottage Doors*

his friend and mentor and most of the founder members were based in London, leaving Gainsborough geographically remote from the Academy and therefore easily marginalized. Perhaps the most potent evidence of his enduring discomfort, even an admission of his disloyalty, was that he chose to be buried nearby Kirby in the churchyard of St Anne's, Kew, when he died thirty years later (figs. 7 and 8).

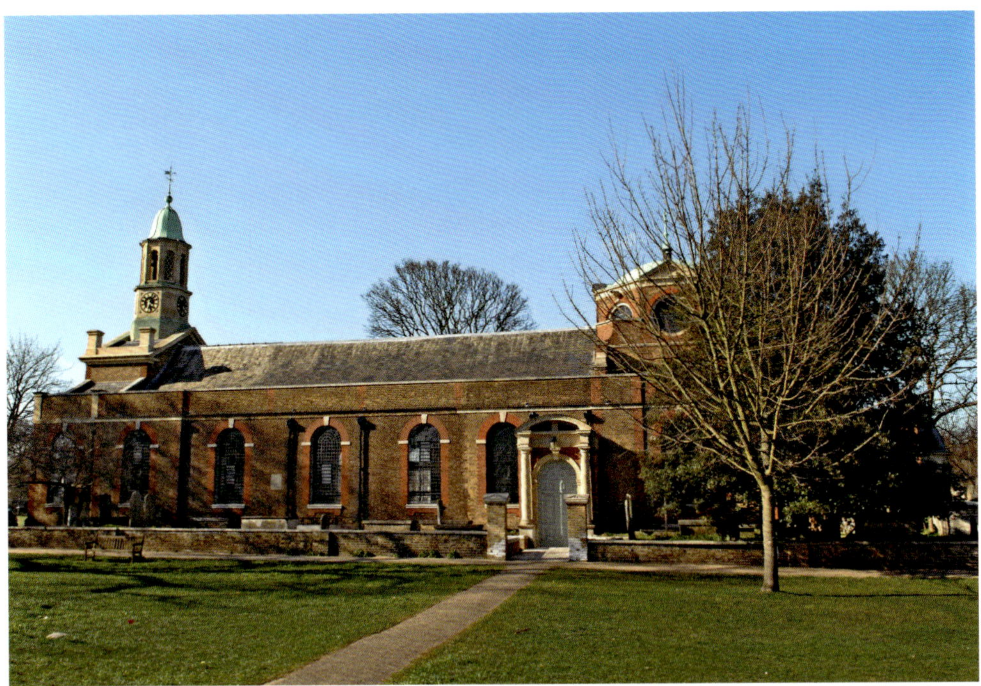

Notes

1   Ann Bermingham, *Sensation & Sensibility: Viewing Gainsborough's Cottage Door*, New Haven and London 2005. *Gainsborough's Landscapes: Themes and Variations* was staged at the Holburne Museum from 24 September 2011 until 8 January 2012 and a reduced version was shown at Compton Verney, Warwickshire, from February to June 2012.

2   Appropriately the resulting painting is now in the Louvre. See Michael Rosenthal, *The Art of Thomas Gainsborough: a little business for the Eye*, New Haven and London 1999, pp. 126–27, pl. 118 col.; Hugh Belsey, *Gainsborough: A Country Life*, London 2002, pp. 17–18 repr. col.

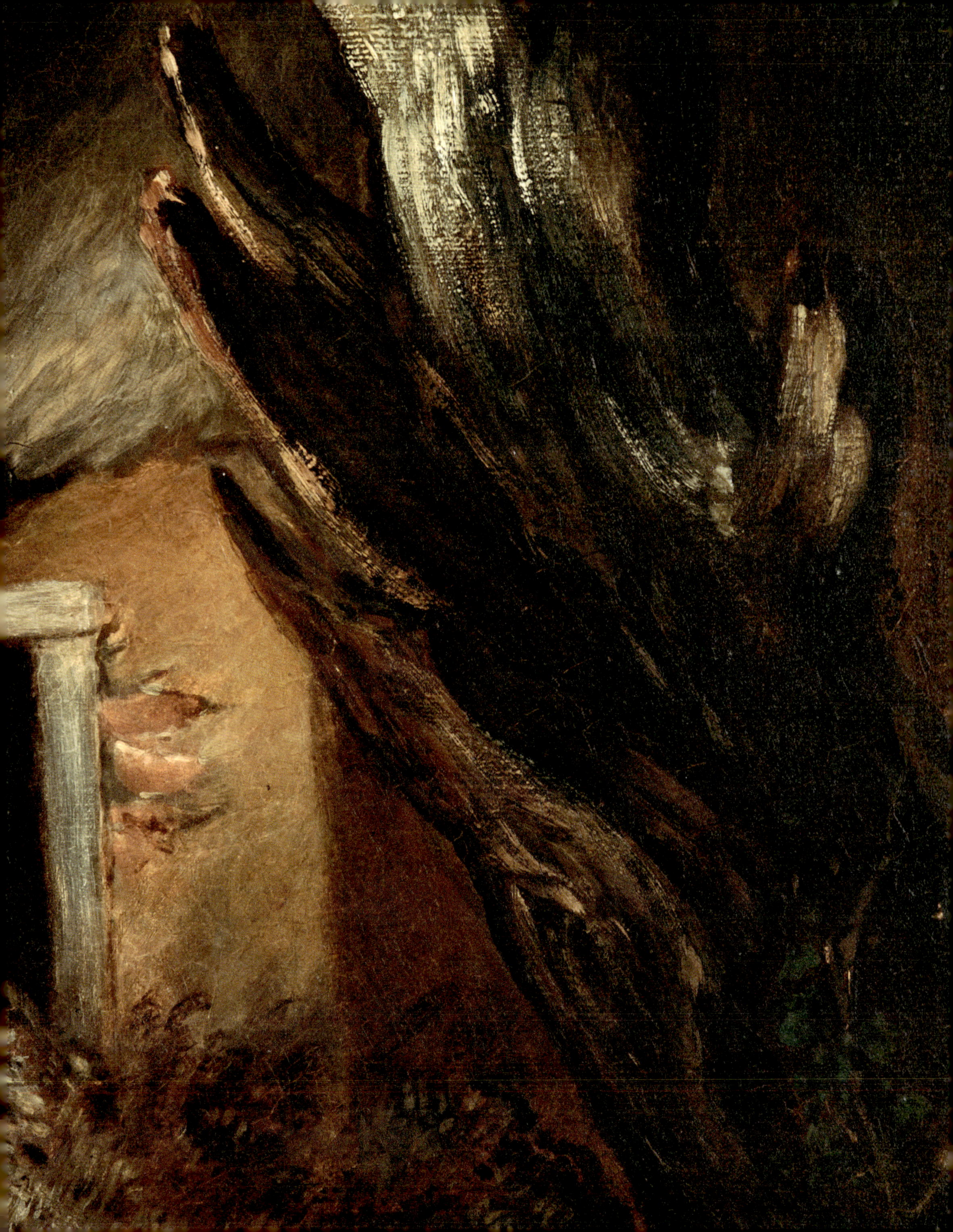

"He never more, whilst he breaths, will send another Picture to the Exhibition"

ON 22 JUNE 1773 Thomas Gainsborough wrote to the Duke of
Kingston's steward, Mr Whatley at Bradford-upon-Avon, giving
"notice … to quit the Duke of Kingston's House in the Abby
Church yard Bath, at Christmas next".[1] The large house had been
leased by Gainsborough from the Duke of Kingston's estate from
Midsummer Day 1760 initially for seven years, an agreement he
renewed for a further seven years in 1767. During his stay in the
city he also took property outside "the smoake" in Lansdown in
the mid 1760s for health reasons and later in the decade he became
one of the first tenants of a house in the newly built Circus, half
a mile up the hill to the north of the old city. Nonetheless, the
Duke of Kingston's house was the property with which he was
most closely associated and where he provided the public with an
exhibition of his paintings.[2] So the ending of the lease on the large
Abbey Churchyard house would have been a significant moment
and it must have helped him come to the decision that he should
leave the city for pastures new.

One gains the impression that as the decade progressed
Gainsborough had fallen out of sympathy with Bath. The Irish
artist John Warren wrote a letter from Bath dated 23 November
1776 to his friend in Dublin, a member of the Irish Parliament,
Andrew Caldwell, that the "good nature" that Gainsborough
reputedly enjoyed was misplaced "as he was uncommonly rude
& uncivil to artists in general, & even haughty to his employers,
which with his proud prices caus'd him to settle in London".[3]
Warren was implying that Gainsborough was finding, in the
artist's words, the "Tea drinkings, Dancings, Husband huntings"
of Bath small-minded and constraining, and, furthermore, Joseph
Wright of Derby had received several reports that the city was
suffering from "a want of business [which] was the reason for
Gainsborough's leaving Bath".[4]

Fourteen years earlier, Gainsborough's move from Ipswich had been carefully prepared, with a visit in the autumn of 1758 to see whether the plan to move to the West Country was worthwhile, a return to Ipswich in the following spring to settle affairs in Suffolk and the final move to Bath with his family in the autumn of 1759.[5] He had arrived in the city at exactly the right moment. For reasons that have never been fully explained, there was a huge demand for portraits in the early 1760s. During the first half of the decade he was never busier and such a heavy workload provided him with the opportunity to establish his name and increase his reputation. Sadly, however, he overworked, ending up with a debilitating illness during the autumn of 1763 that took him out of his studio for several months.[6]

As Gainsborough settled in Bath, the Society of Artists was arranging its first public exhibition. Gainsborough had nothing available for the first display in 1760 but he exhibited annually thereafter, carefully choosing portraits and landscapes to show the quality and range of his ability. Gainsborough was never interested in artistic politics and whenever possible he kept them at arms' length. Furthermore, as we have already mentioned, his personal loyalty made him regard the manoeuverings against his friend and mentor Joshua Kirby, the President of the Society of Artists, during the founding of the Royal Academy of Arts in 1768 as underhand. Nonetheless he realised that he had no choice but to accept the offer of membership of the Academy when the invitation came late in 1768, though he always regarded it with suspicion, and was obliged to resign his directorship of the Society of Artists.[7] His dissatisfaction increased with time and the views of its President, Sir Joshua Reynolds, detailed in annual Discourses delivered to the Academy's students each December and published shortly afterwards, were a growing concern for

Gainsborough. He clearly regarded this unchecked platform as a serious threat to proper discussion and wrote of his unease to his friend and fellow artist in Bath, William Hoare, a man twenty years his senior and a long-established portraitist.

Hoare had lent Gainsborough a copy of the Discourse that Reynolds had delivered to the students of the Royal Academy on 10 December 1772, and Gainsborough responded in a heartfelt letter early the next year. Conscious that Hoare, like Reynolds, had learned much during his time in Italy, Gainsborough begins by hedging his bets, praising the Discourse as "amazingly clever, and cannot be too much admired (together with its Ingenious Author) by every candid lover of the Art. The truth of what He observes concerning Fresco, and the Great Style, Mr G. is convinced of by what he has often heard Mr Hoare say of the works of Raffaelle & Michel Angelo."

Gainsborough then continues in more critical vein, raging against the impracticalities of Reynolds' suggestions,

– but betwixt Friends Sir Joshua either forgets, or does not chuse [to] see that his Instruction is all adapted to form the History Painter, which he must know there is no call for in this country. The Ornamental Style (as he calls it) seems form'd for Portraits. Therefore he had better come down to Watteau at once (who was a very fine Painter taking away the French conceit) and let us have a few Tints: or Else why does Sir Joshua put tints equal to Painted Glass, only to make the People talk of Colors flying, when the great style would do – every one knows that the grand Style must consist in plainness & simplicity, and that silks & satins Pearls & trifling ornaments would be as hurtfull to simplicity, as flourishes in a Psalm Tune; but Fresco would no more do for Portraits, than an Organ would please Ladies in the hands of Fischer; there

must be Variety of lively touches and surprizing Effects to
make the Heart dance, or else they had better be in a Church –
so in Portrait Painting there must be a Lustre and finishing to
bring it up to individual Life.

Gainsborough ends his letter by saying that he "hopes to talk over
the Affair some evening over a Glass, as there is no other Friendly
or Sensible way of settling these matters except upon Canvass".[8]

Whatever the result of these discussions, Gainsborough
came to the conclusion that the market he served had no use
for history painting. His work was based on the traditions of
portraiture and landscape painting and showed little regard
for classical or religious subject matter. He saw little future in
supporting an institution that propagated ideas contrary to his
own, and he did not want his work to be found wanting by the
Academy because of the subjects he chose. He did not submit
anything for exhibition at the Royal Academy in 1773. His
conversation with Hoare also made him realise that Reynolds's
Discourses were a further indication that any ambitious artist
must move to London if his opinions were to be regarded with
any degree of seriousness. Consequently he planned his future
strategies carefully.

In May 1774, shortly before he left Bath, flaunting the
regulations that restricted Royal Academicians from exhibiting
anywhere but the Academy, he appears to have shown a portrait
of Lord Mountmorres at the Free Society of Artists (fig. 9).[9]
The portrait, now in a private collection, is a simple head and
shoulders, not painted for show, but its exhibition no doubt
marked a degree of dissatisfaction – a sense of shifting allegiance
– and it also heralded his move to London.

From Midsummer Day 1774 Gainsborough rented for £150
per annum the western third of Schomberg House from a fellow

FIG. 9
Thomas Gainsborough
Lord Mountmorres, exhibited at
the Free Society of Artists 1774
Oil on canvas, 76.2 × 63.5 cm
Private collection

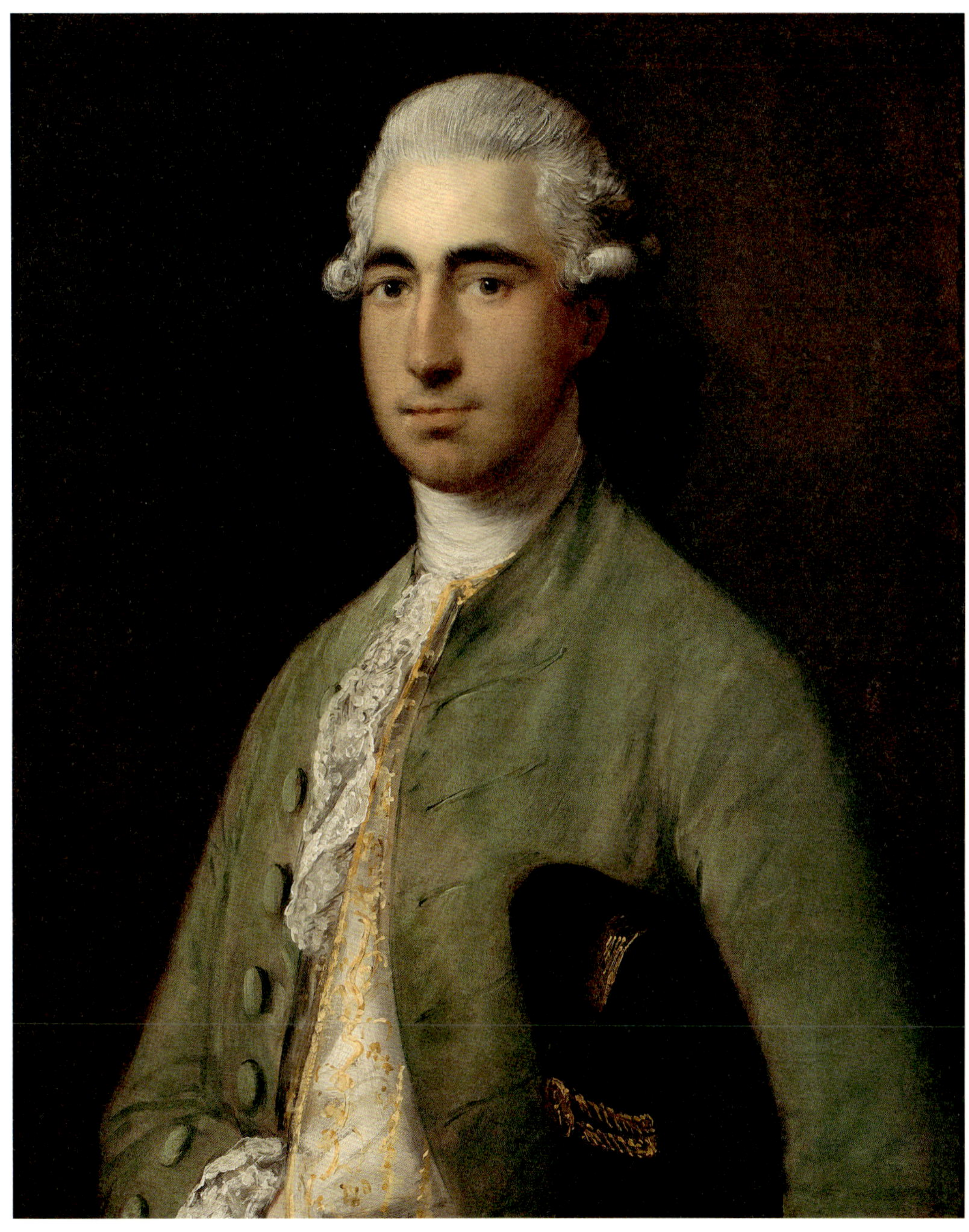

artist, John Astley. Astley, realising the potential of the building, had converted the property into a terrace of three dwellings in 1769 and taken the central portion for himself. Gainsborough appreciated the potential too. The position was perfect, located in Pall Mall close to St James's Palace, adjacent to James Christie's auction rooms, and near the Great Room, Spring Gardens, where the Society of Artists held their annual exhibition – and, at least until 1780, further along the street the building known until 1767 as Dalton's Print Warehouse hosted the Royal Academy's exhibitions.[10] Gainsborough had chosen to settle in the centre of the artistic community with future clients, courtiers, visitors to the Academy exhibitions and buyers at the auctioneer's all close at hand.

It is not known whether he had had contact with the court before his move to London, but within nine months Gainsborough had achieved some recognition from royalty. On 24 April the *Morning Chronicle* noted that "The Duke and Duchess of Gloucester are often going to a famous painter's in Pall-mall; and 'tis reported that he is now doing both their pictures, which are intended to be presented to a Great Lady". The author misidentified the sitters, who were in fact another brother of George III, Henry, Duke of Cumberland, and his recent bride Anne, the widow of Christopher Horton. Gainsborough had first met and painted Anne Horton in 1766 (Dublin, National Gallery of Ireland) and she may have introduced the duke to the painter.[11]

The full-length portraits of the Cumberlands, now in the Royal Collection (figs. 11, 12), were intended for a new house designed by Robert Adam in Portman Square for Elizabeth, Dowager Countess of Home, which was then in the final stages of completion (fig. 10).[12] Not surprisingly, these were not the only portraits he was painting at the time.

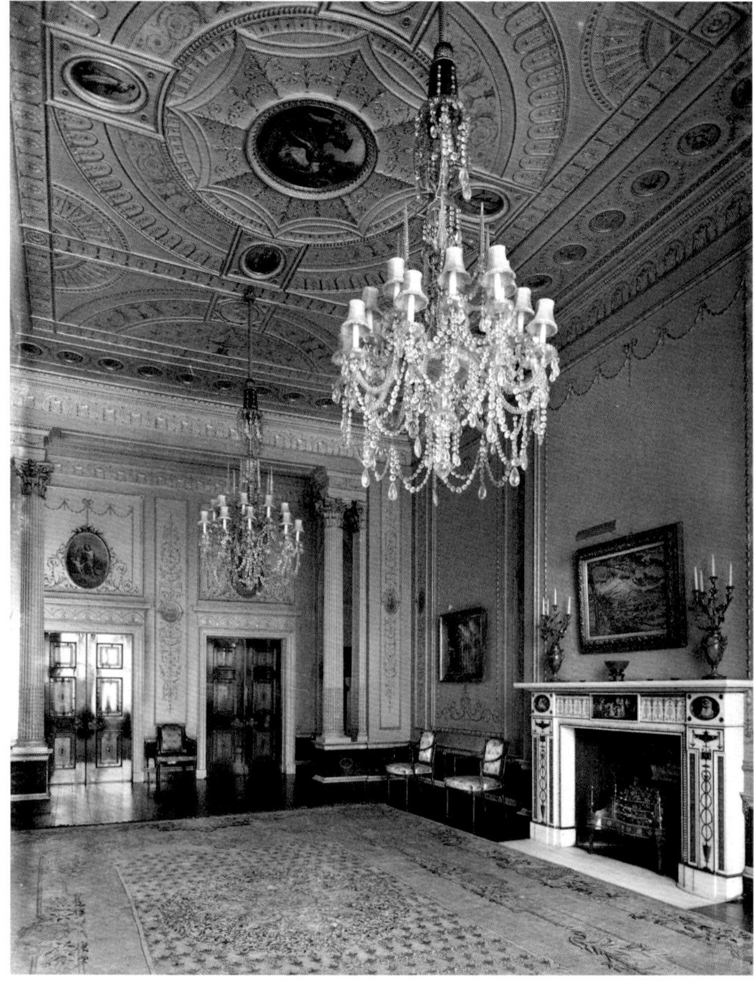

On 26 December 1774 the Hon. Mary Cathcart married
Thomas Graham at her father's house in Grosvenor Place,
London, and, at the same ceremony, her elder sister Jane married
John, Duke of Atholl. Mary Graham was regarded as a great
beauty and Gainsborough must have been quick to take the
opportunity to paint her before she left London and travelled
to her husband's estates in Perthshire. She briefly returned to
London before visiting another of her sisters, Louisa, Lady
Mansfield, in Paris the following summer, a visit which may
have provided a further opportunity for her to sit to the artist.

All the indications are that the portrait was not commissioned
by the sitter but painted to exhibit at Schomberg House to serve

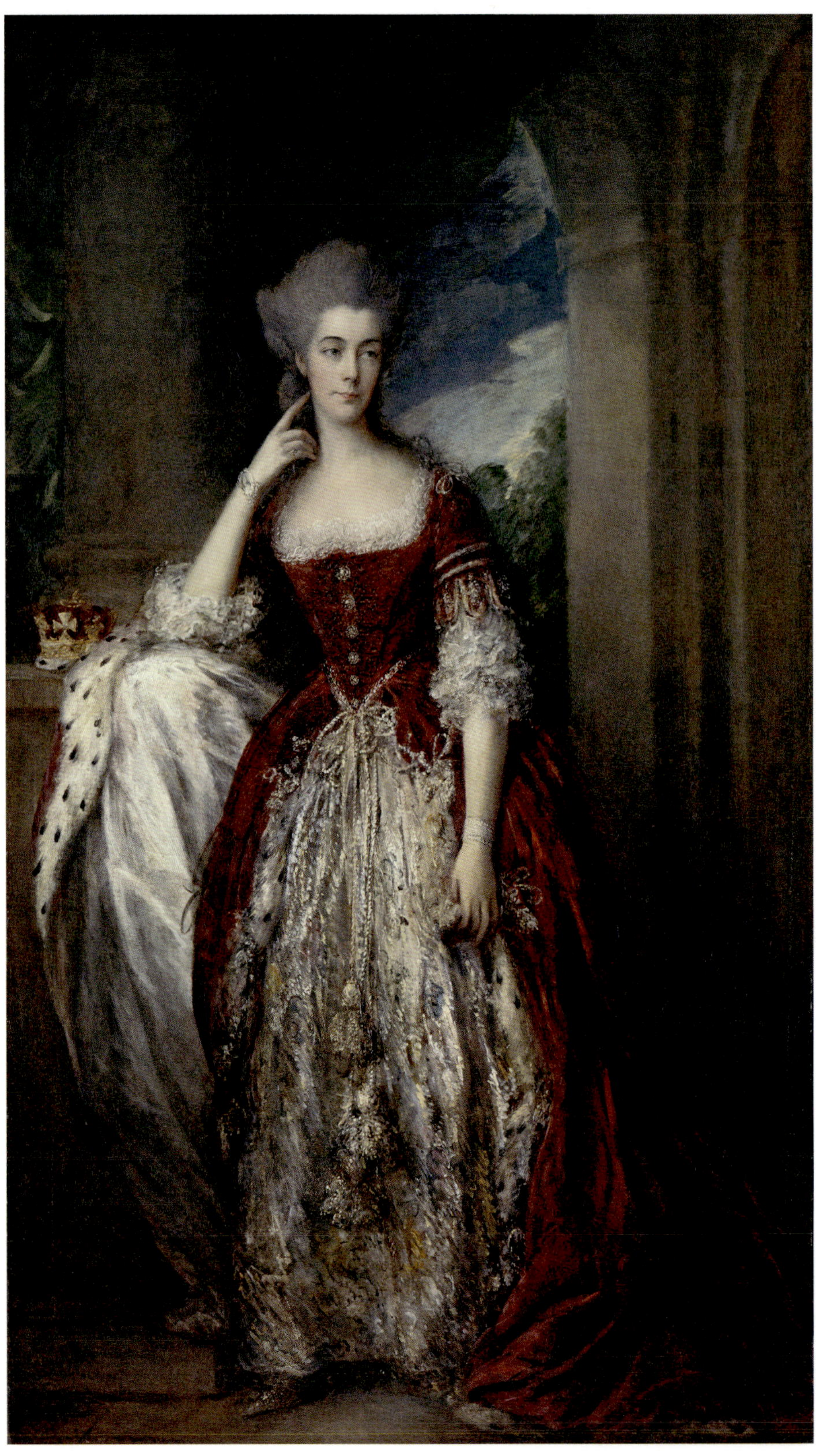

FIG. 11
Thomas Gainsborough
Anne, Duchess of Cumberland, 1773–77
Oil on canvas, 238.1 × 142.2 cm
Royal Collection

*Gainsborough's
Cottage Doors*

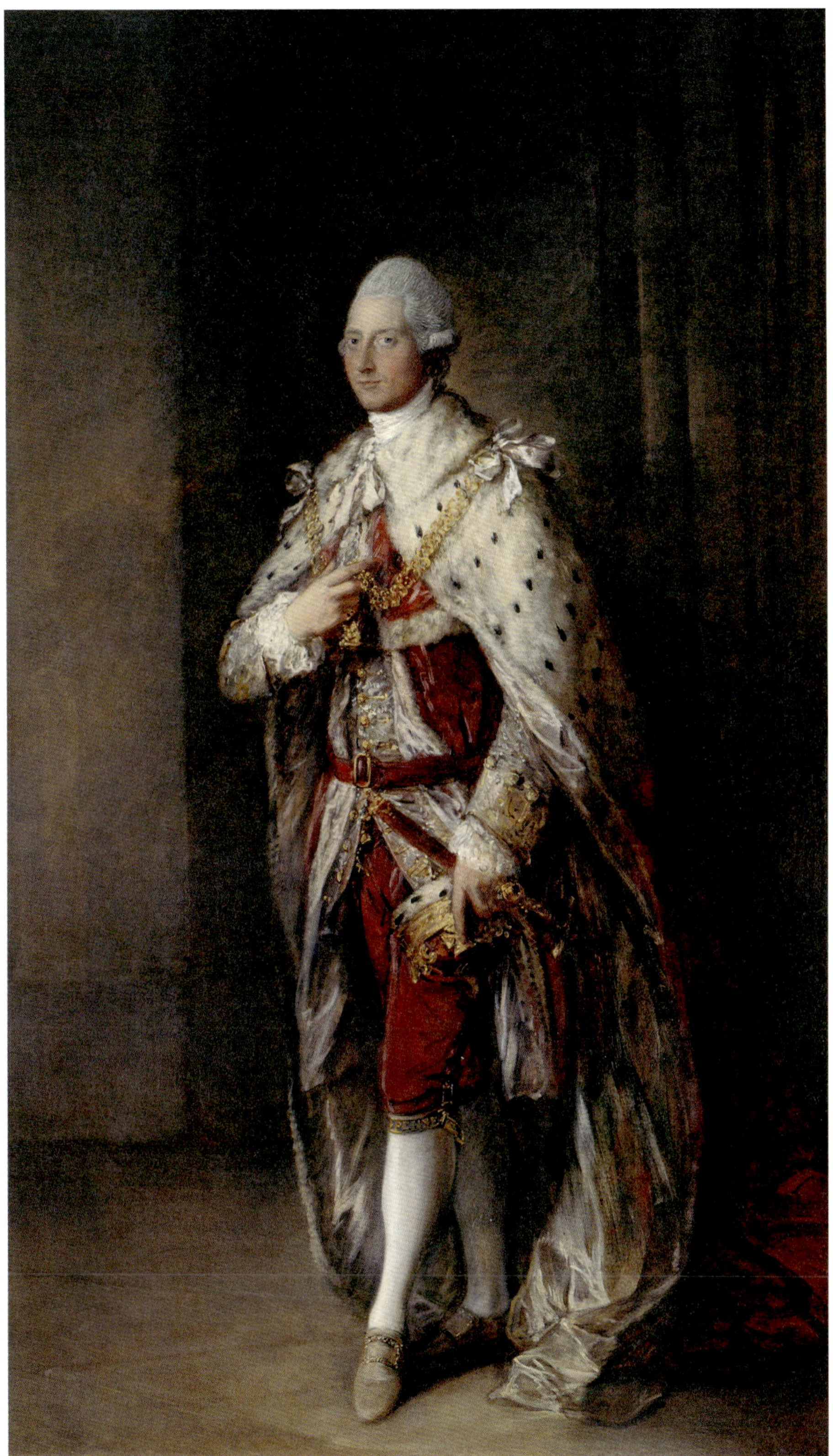

Thomas Gainsborough
Henry, Duke of Cumberland, 1773–77
Oil on canvas, 238.1 × 142.2 cm
Royal Collection

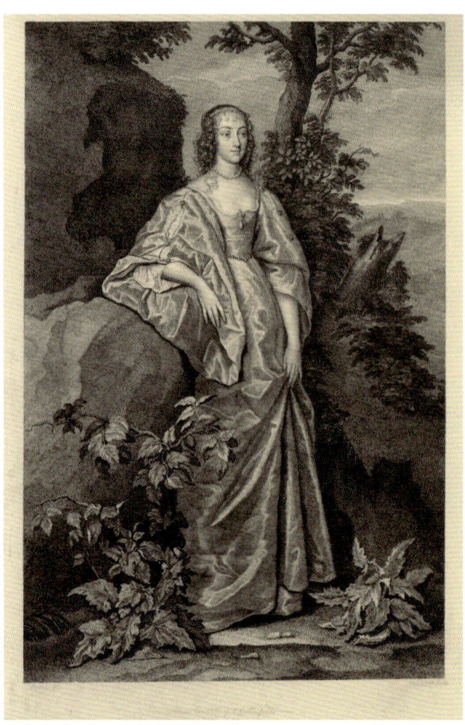

*Gainsborough's
Cottage Doors*

as an advertisement of Gainsborough's ability. Given Reynolds's emphasis on the pre-eminence of the Italian school of painting in his Discourses, Gainsborough deliberately adopted an opposing stance, followed his own instincts and chose to paint the portrait in the style of Van Dyck.

Sir Anthony van Dyck's portraits had particular resonance in England. He had been the most adept artist to paint the English aristocracy and he had developed an elegance in appearance and an easy confidence in attitude that admirably matched the style of his sitters. This formula had created the vocabulary for later portraiture in Britain. Furthermore, by the second half of the eighteenth century, with its volatile politics and the creation of many new peerages, sitters in Van Dyck dress provided a sense of continuity and a reassuring link to the ancient order before Commonwealth and Restoration. Van Dyck's deft handling of paint, characterization and sumptuous colouring sparked the innate abilities of Gainsborough's artistry and, with so much in common, Van Dyck became the natural mentor for the eighteenth-century artist. Gainsborough's visual resourcefulness and his faultless draughtsmanship provided him with the ability to make the visual connection with Van Dyck a uniquely fruitful one.

Gainsborough chose to mirror the pose of Van Dyck's portrait of Lady Chesterfield in his canvas of Mrs Graham (fig. 14).[13] Before being purchased by Lord Radnor, Van Dyck's portrait had been on the London art market in the first half of 1773. Later in the same year Gainsborough visited Longford Castle to paint a series of head-and-shoulder portraits of members of the Radnor family and the visit gave him ample opportunity to see the newly acquired portrait and other works in the castle. Radnor's generosity in making his growing collection readily available enabled Gainsborough to paint two copies of a landscape

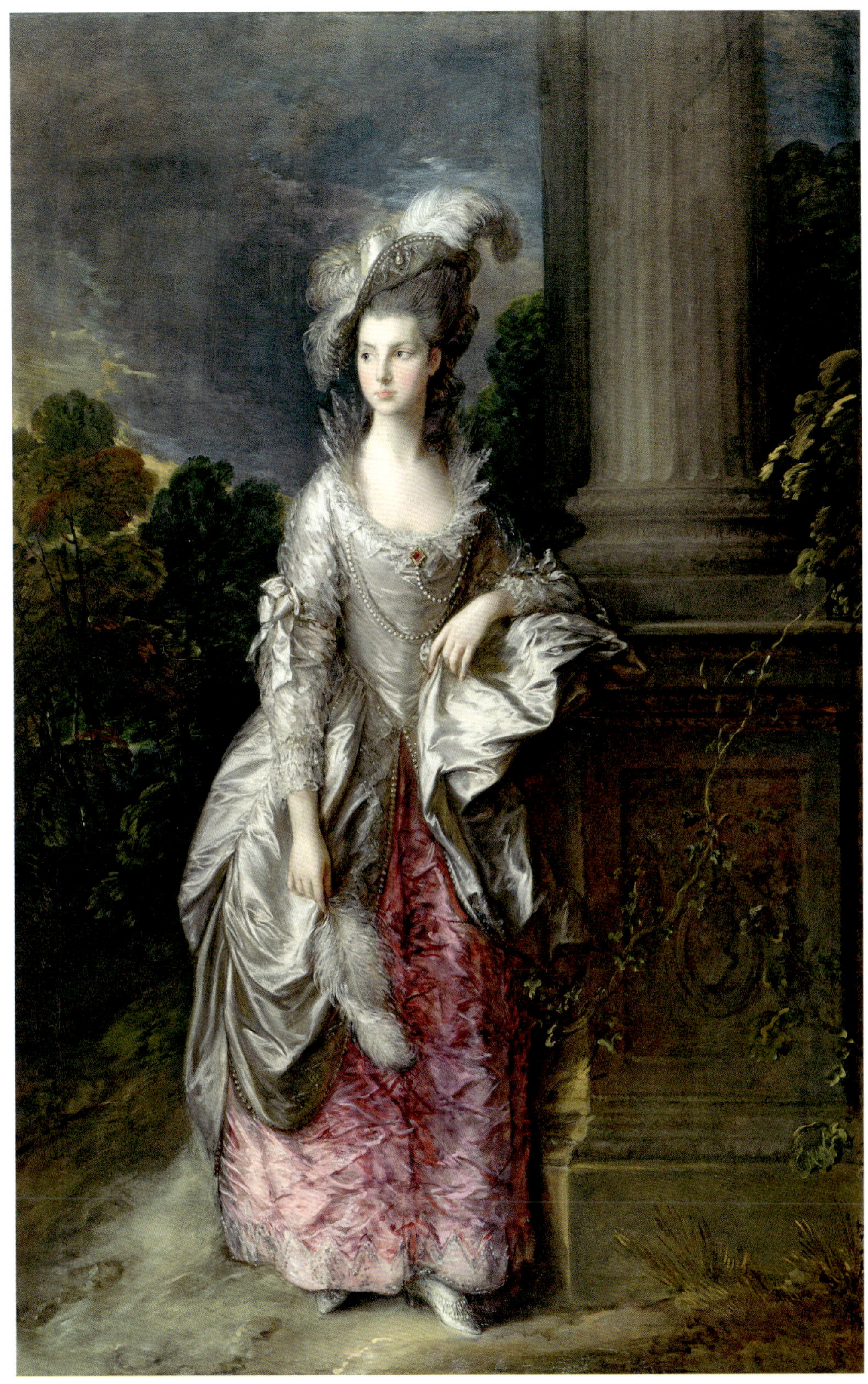

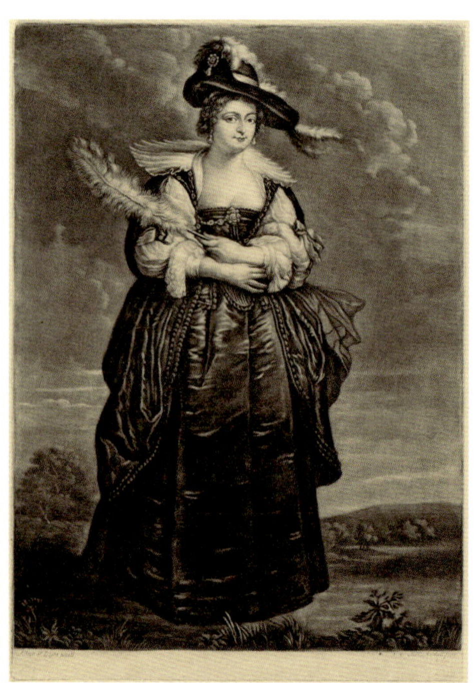

FIG. 15
James McArdell after Peter Paul Rubens
Hélène Fourment, before 1765
Mezzotint, 354 × 252 mm
British Museum, London

Gainsborough's
Cottage Doors

by David Teniers (Dublin, National Gallery of Ireland and private collection).[14] Although no copy by Gainsborough of Van Dyck's Lady Chesterfield is known, the artist probably owned an impression of the engraving of the portrait by Pieter van Gunst, published in 1636, and he could have referred to this in his studio in London (fig. 13).

The costume, as well as the pose, are based on prototypes by Van Dyck. Mary Graham's hat is adapted from one worn by Hélène Fourment in a portrait then owned by the Earl of Orford at Houghton Hall in Norfolk. The painting had been popularized in a mezzotint scraped by James McArdell sometime in the late 1750s or early 1760s (fig. 15) with an inscription describing it (erroneously) as a painting by Van Dyck and in 1767 a further mezzotint was also scraped by Louis Sailliar. During the eighteenth century it was considered to be amongst Van Dyck's greatest works, though now it is recognized as a painting by Sir Peter Paul Rubens. Having been purchased from Houghton by Catherine the Great, it remained in St Petersburg for one hundred and fifty years, then was sold to Calouste Gulbenkian in the 1930s: it is now in the Fundação Calouste Gulbenkian in Lisbon (fig. 16).[15] Like Gainsborough's portrait known as the 'Blue Boy', exhibited at the Royal Academy in 1770, the portrait of Mrs Graham was intended as a headstrong demonstration of Gainsborough's unique ability to outdo Van Dyck.

On 28 April, four days after the press had mentioned the Royal Duke and Duchess sitting to Gainsborough, the artist's name reappeared in the newspapers. In a notice of that year's Royal Academy exhibition, the *Public Advertiser* commented that the show "cuts a very respectable Figure, considering there are several eminent Artists belonging to the Academy who have exhibited nothing this Year, viz. Mess. *Dance, Gainsborough and Cipriani*".[16]

FIG. 16
Peter Paul Rubens
Hélène Fourment, 1630–32
Oil on panel, 186 × 85 cm
Fundação Calouste Gulbenkian,
Lisbon

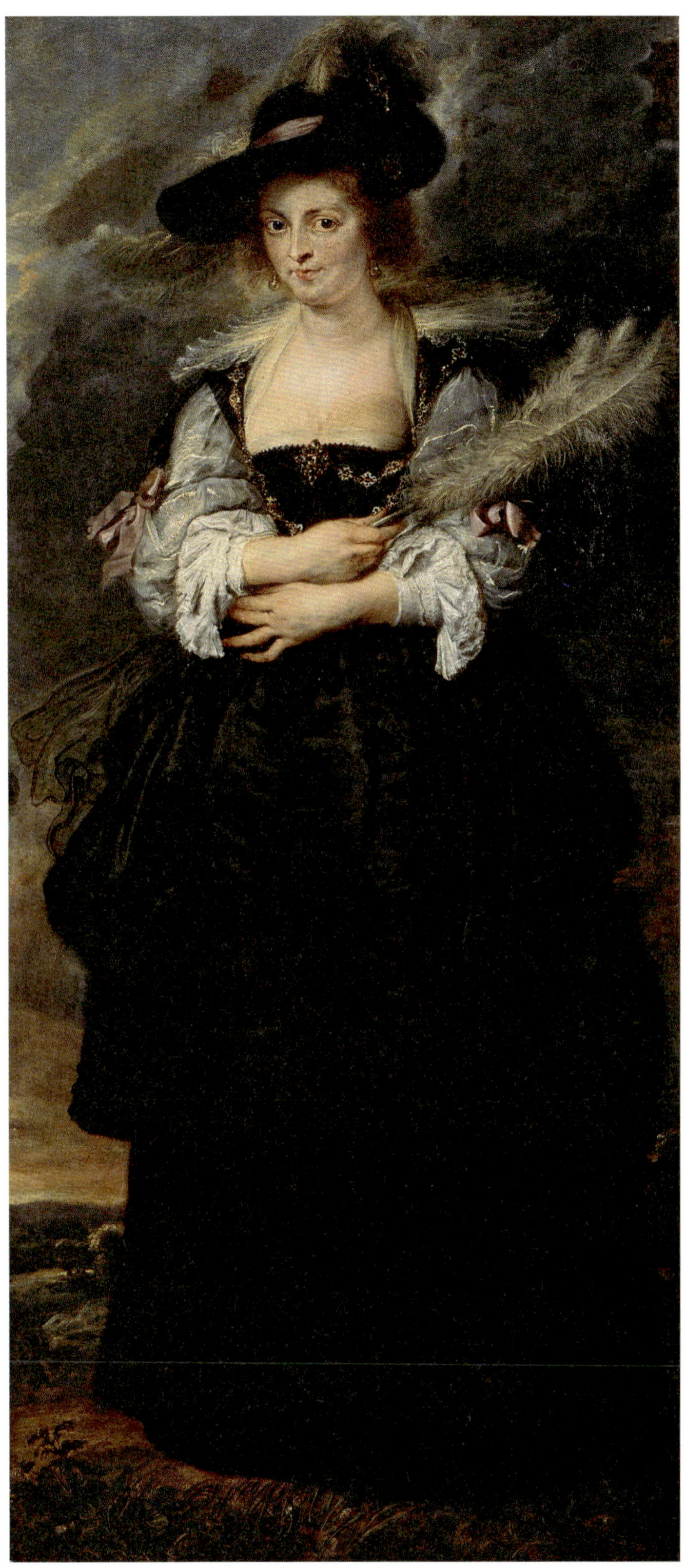

A correspondent in the *Morning Chronicle* was more critical:
"I am sorry to observe that the Exhibition of the Royal Academy
is much fallen off this year; there is a great miss of some principal
artists; Dance, Cipriani, Gainsborough, and Hone are wanting,
and even those who have exhibited are very short of their former
excellence".[17]

Nathaniel Dance, one of the artists mentioned in the list,
had been unwell in 1774 and around the same time his finances
had changed for the better. Although the source of his wealth is
unknown, he appears to have become financially independent
and he no longer needed to rely on income from portrait
commissions. Dance had been a pupil of Francis Hayman in
London between 1752 and 1754, when he must have come to
know Gainsborough. Sadly, if there was any correspondence
between the two artists it has been long since disappeared, but it
is reasonable to assume that the two artists had respect for each
other and had kept in touch. In 1754 Dance had travelled to Italy,
where he had developed his skill as a history painter, an activity
he did not pursue once he returned to England, preferring, like so
many of his contemporaries, to develop a portrait practice. Like
Gainsborough Dance had had misgivings about the Academy
and failed to submit any exhibits for the 1773 exhibition, although
his work may have been absent from the 1775 display owing to
illness. Given his early interest in history painting Dance had
respect for the aims of the Academy, while he also must have had
some sympathy with his friend of twenty-five years' standing.
Consequently he was nominated to discuss Gainsborough's
concerns on the Academy's behalf, with the intention of
persuading him to reconsider his position.

The conversation was clearly a success, as Gainsborough
agreed to exhibit his work at the Academy in 1777. On 26 April

the *Public Advertiser* wrote, "We are glad to see *Mr. Gainsborough* once more submitting his Performances to public Inspection; which cannot fail to add to the Entertainment of the Town, as well as to the Reputation and Emolument of the Artist: 'Tis hard to say in which Branch of the Art Mr. Gainsborough most excels, Landscape or Portrait Painting: Let the Connoisseurs carefully examine the portrait of Mr. *Abel* … or the large Landscape … and then determine – if they can!"

The portrait of Carl Friedrich Abel (fig. 18), a close friend of the artist and the greatest viola da gamba player of his generation, was perhaps intended for the rooms in Hanover Square where Abel had organized a series of subscription concerts with his fellow musician Johann Christian Bach. The portrait is indeed remarkable and a journalist writing in the *Morning Post* on 25 April thought that it was "the finest modern portrait we remember to have seen". The landscape, known as *The Watering Place*, is now in the National Gallery, London (fig. 17), and when he saw it in the exhibition Horace Walpole described it as "by far the finest Landscape ever painted in England".[18] The portraits of Mrs Graham and the Cumberlands were also included in the exhibition and by the very fact that he could choose the best of his work painted during the previous four years Gainsborough gained an appreciable advantage over his rivals.

In 1780 the Academy moved into the north wing of Somerset House, into rooms now occupied by the Courtauld Institute Galleries, which was a further affirmation of official approval for the organization and a move that shifted the artistic centre of the capital from Pall Mall further east, towards the City (fig. 19). Gainsborough continued to exhibit at the Academy and to build his reputation through the press. His friendship with Henry Bate (later Revd Sir Henry Bate-Dudley), a maverick parson, huntsman

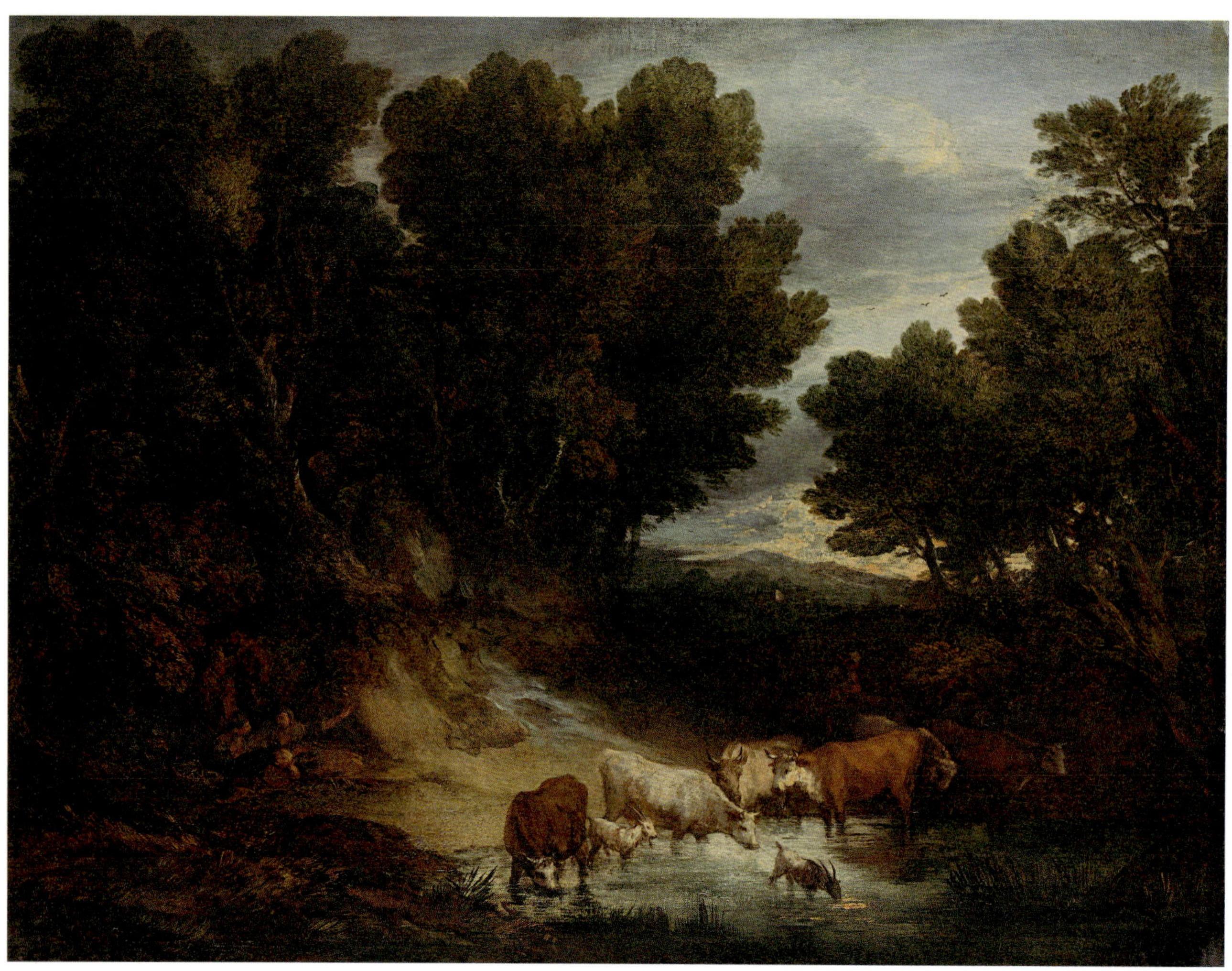

FIG.17
Thomas Gainsborough
The Watering Place, exhibited 1777
Oil on canvas, 147.3 × 180.3 cm
National Gallery, London

FIG. 18
Thomas Gainsborough
Carl Friedrich Abel, exhibited 1777
Oil on canvas, 225.4 × 151.1 cm
The Huntington Library, Art Collections,
and Botanical Gardens, San Marino

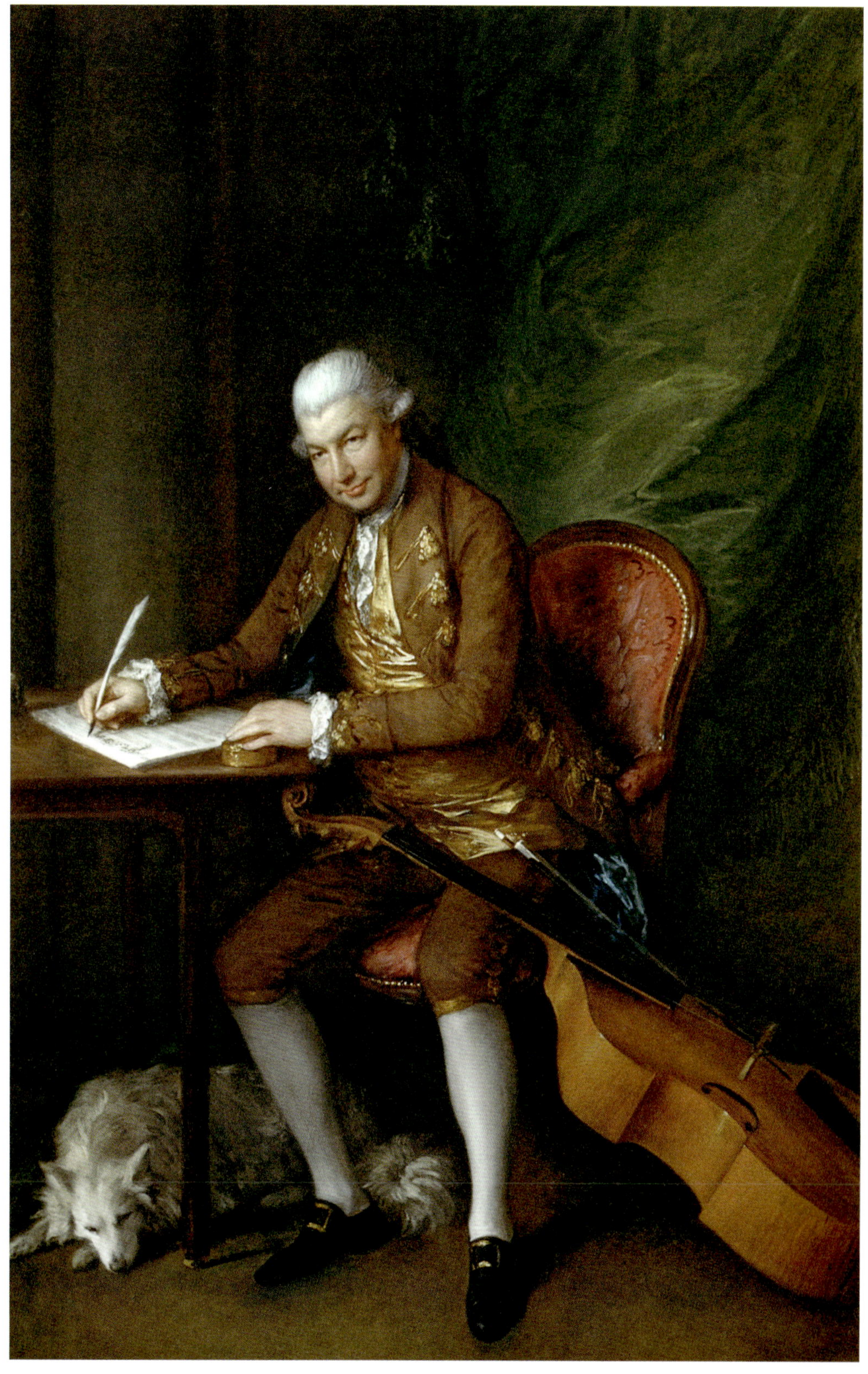

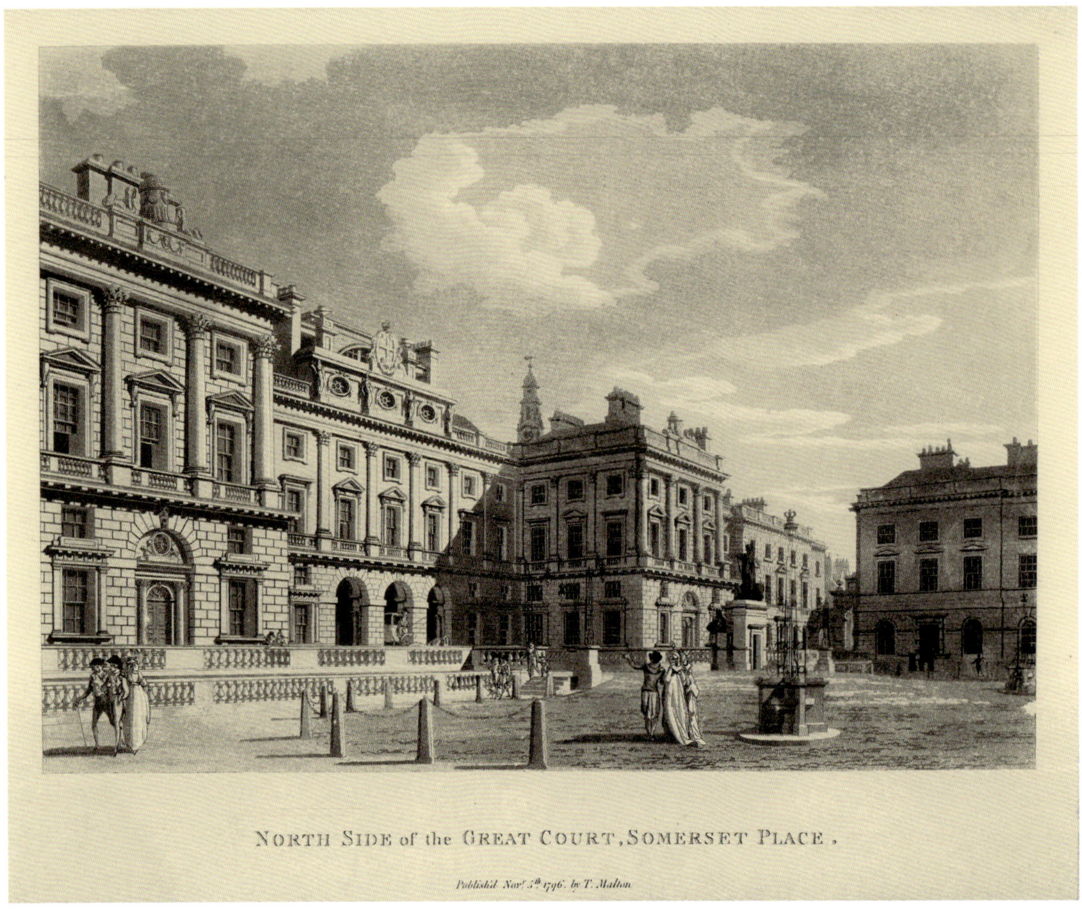

Gainsborough's
Cottage Doors

and newspaper proprietor, was especially useful. In November 1780 Bate launched the *Morning Herald*, and Gainsborough began to feed him snippets about his activities that appear to have been printed verbatim. Obviously frustrated by the expectations and the constraints on his artistic activity, Gainsborough began to experiment around 1780, painting a number of seascapes. The two that he exhibited in 1781 prompted Bate to write, "Mr. Gainsborough's two sea-views, shew the universality of his genius; for though they are his first attempts in this line, the water is exquisitely painted!"[19] The condition of one of these sea-views, reputedly painted for Richard Grosvenor, whose descendents still own it, has been examined in a conservation studio, where it was discovered that the painter had painstakingly built up and rubbed down layers of paint to produce an exceptional effect of the sea in

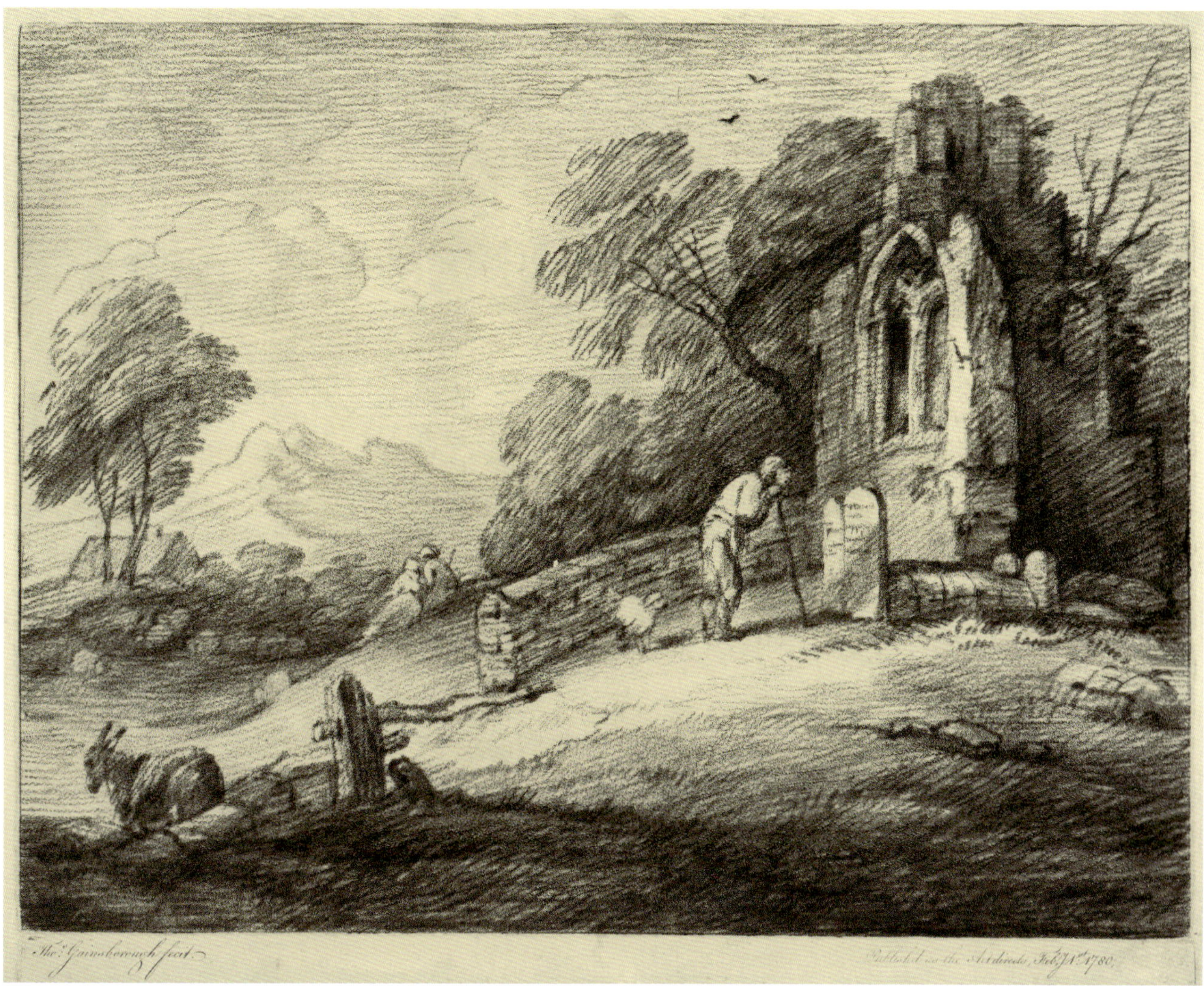

a squall with waves crashing against the beach.[20] Gainsborough also turned his mind to printmaking. Using soft-ground etching and aquatint on three large copper plates he formed three complementary landscapes. The method was designed to imitate chalk-and-wash drawings, media that he favoured at the time. The three prints were each dated 1 February 1780 and one bears a signature (fig. 20). Perhaps the intention was for the other two to be signed as well. Enticingly, following the date all three have a space where a word of eight or nine letters has been erased.[21] For whatever reason, they were never published and remain amongst the rarest prints produced in eighteenth-century England.

FIG. 20
Thomas Gainsborough
Peasant reading a tombstone, 1780
Soft-ground etching and
aquatint, 297 × 394 mm
The Huntington Library, Art
Collections, and Botanical Gardens,
San Marino. Gift of Norman Baker
of Evans, Pierson & Co.

These rare prints were as experimental as the oil seascapes.
They represent one of the first uses of aquatint, a technique
that Gainsborough probably learned from another of his long-
standing professional friends, Paul Sandby. As Michael Rosenthal
has described,[22] they make reference to landscapes by Old Masters
and represent the variety of landscape paintings that occupied
Gainsborough's imagination at the time. The project may well
have been an aborted experiment in self-advertisement with which
the artist hoped to popularize his landscape practice.

Also in the 1781 exhibition Gainsborough showed *A shepherd*,
a study of a lad, frightened and vulnerable, accompanied by his
dog, sheltering under a tree during a storm. Reynolds was to
describe the genre as a 'fancy picture' and it was in many regards
a detail of the staffage from one of Gainsborough's landscapes
enlarged to become the subject of a canvas. More importantly
it was Gainsborough attempting to make a self-contained
painting, independent of portraiture, that could be considered
a contemporary old master – a modern 'history painting' – to
be regarded on its own merits. The intention was to exert some
'sentiment', to use the word in its eighteenth-century meaning,
in the heart of the beholder so that the viewer felt some empathy
for the shepherd boy and his faithful dog.

Contemporary critics admired the work. Henry Bate in
the *Morning Herald* on 1 May 1781 wrote, "the *Shepherd Boy* in
a tempestuous scene, is evidently the *chef d'oeuvre* of this great
artist, a composition in which the numberless beauties of design,
drawing, and colouring, are so admirably blended as to excite the
admiration of every beholder!" The author in *St James's Chronicle*
on 10 May 1781 was rather bemused by the painting, although it
had "met with Approbation of the Publick … I must endeavour to
find out from what it proceeds … the Face is handsome, and the

Colouring beautiful and true. The Hands and Feet however should
be more finished, to make this Picture complete." The *London
Chronicle* (28 April–1 May 1781) was less circumspect and felt that
"a Shepherd [was] equal to any picture produced by any modern
artist, and superior to most".[23] The painting was purchased by
Henry Noel, 6th Earl of Gainsborough, but, together with other
canvases by Gainsborough, it was destroyed in a fire at his seat,
Exton Park near Oakham, on 23 May 1810. However, *A shepherd*
is known through a print. Gainsborough was anxious to build
on the popularity of the painting and commissioned a mezzotint
of it from Richard Earlom. Remarkably, a proof of the print with
Gainsborough's alterations survives at Gainsborough's House
(fig. 21) and it shows the detailed concern the artist had in its
production. The same 1781 exhibition included Gainsborough's
portraits of George III and Queen Charlotte, which were to
become replacements for the official likenesses produced by
Allan Ramsay in 1761 and endlessly repeated over the next
twenty years and disseminated throughout the English-speaking
world. Gainsborough must have regarded such royal favour as an
endorsement of his own work and a courtly snub directed towards
the Academy and its President, Sir Joshua Reynolds, who had been
appointed the Principal Painter in Ordinary to the King when he
took up the Presidency of the Academy.

All these changes were of sufficient weight to provide
Gainsborough with the courage to revise his view of the future.
He was confident that the press would support him, he had several
royal commissions under his belt and the new subject-matter he
had adopted had been admired by the public. Already vexed with
frustrations about competitive portrait painting, Gainsborough
must have come to the conclusion that his career could flourish
without the constraints of the Academy.

FIG. 21
Richard Earlom after
Thomas Gainsborough,
retouched by Gainsborough
A shepherd, 1781
Mezzotint with white and
black chalk, 361 × 281 mm
Gainsborough's House, Sudbury

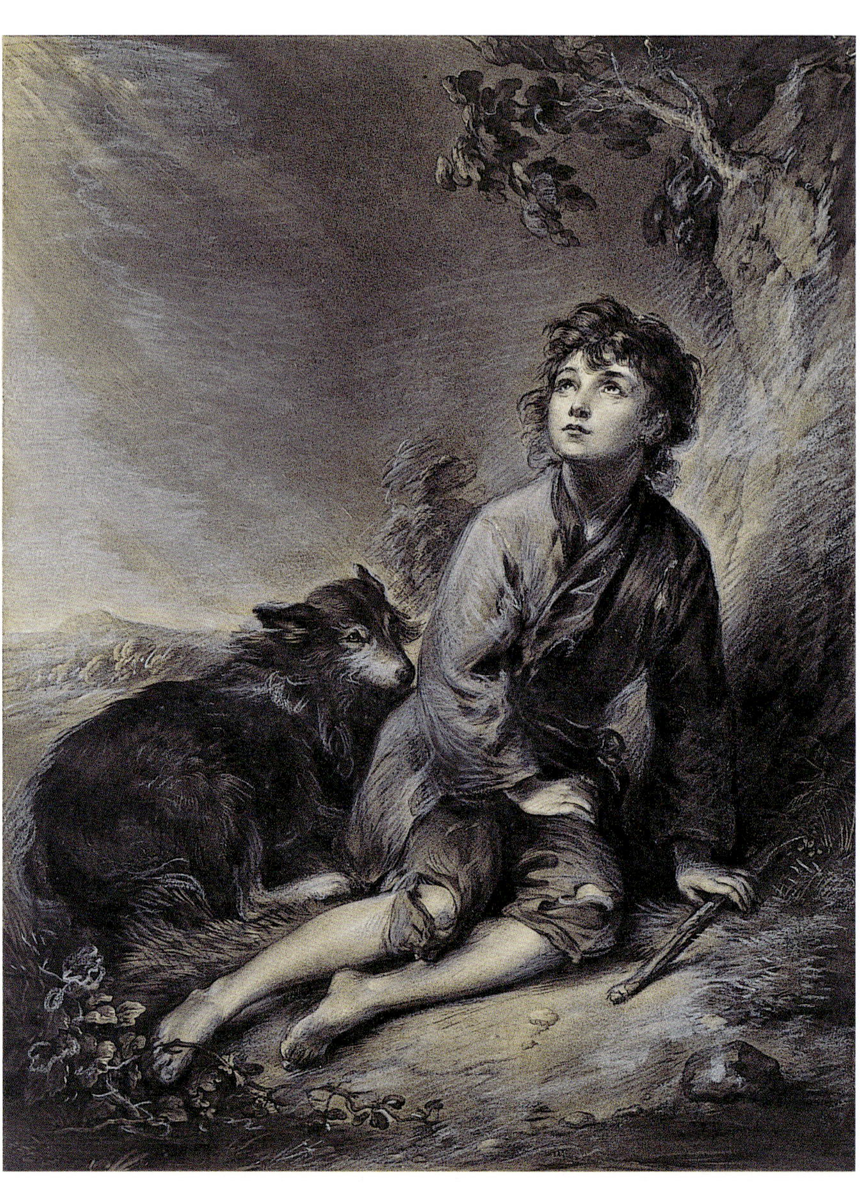

*Gainsborough's
Cottage Doors*

Pleased with the reception of the pair of full-length portraits exhibited in 1781 and beguiled by the personality of the painter, in the autumn of 1782 George III invited Gainsborough to Windsor to paint heads of the whole royal family. True to form, the commission was recorded in the *Morning Herald* on 14 September: "Mr. *Gainsborough* is now down at Windsor painting half length portraits of the whole Royal Family, by command of her Majesty, many of whom he has already finished, in that superior style which has long distinguished his celebrated pencil". They were completed by 30 October, when Bate wrote that the artist "has just completed his painting of the whole Royal Family, at Windsor … all of which are spoken of as highly-finished characteristic portraits of the illustrious personages who sat to him" (fig. 22). To publicize the artist's continuing associations with the court, this series of portraits formed a natural choice to hang in the Royal Academy exhibition the following year.

Perhaps prompted by a query from the Academy, Gainsborough made a sketch explaining the format he wanted for the display of the fifteen royal heads, and he wrote to Francis Milner Newton, the Secretary of the Academy, on the same sheet shortly before the exhibition opened: "I w[d.] beg to have them [the portraits] hung with the Frames touching each other, in this order, the Names are written behind each Picture" (fig. 23).[24] Royal Academy exhibitions were clearly hung at speed, and, in order to fit in as many exhibits on the wall as possible, smaller works were hung 'below the line' – a moulding dressing the walls of the room about nine feet from the ground – while larger works were hung above it, fixed on battens racked out at an angle from the walls. As Edward Francis Burney's drawing shows (fig. 24), by this date exhibits were hung in plain frames packed tightly together.[25] When the frames of the fifteen royal portraits were fixed together

FIG. 22
Thomas Gainsborough
The Royal Family, September 1782
Oil on canvas, each approximately
59 × 43.8 cm
Royal Collection

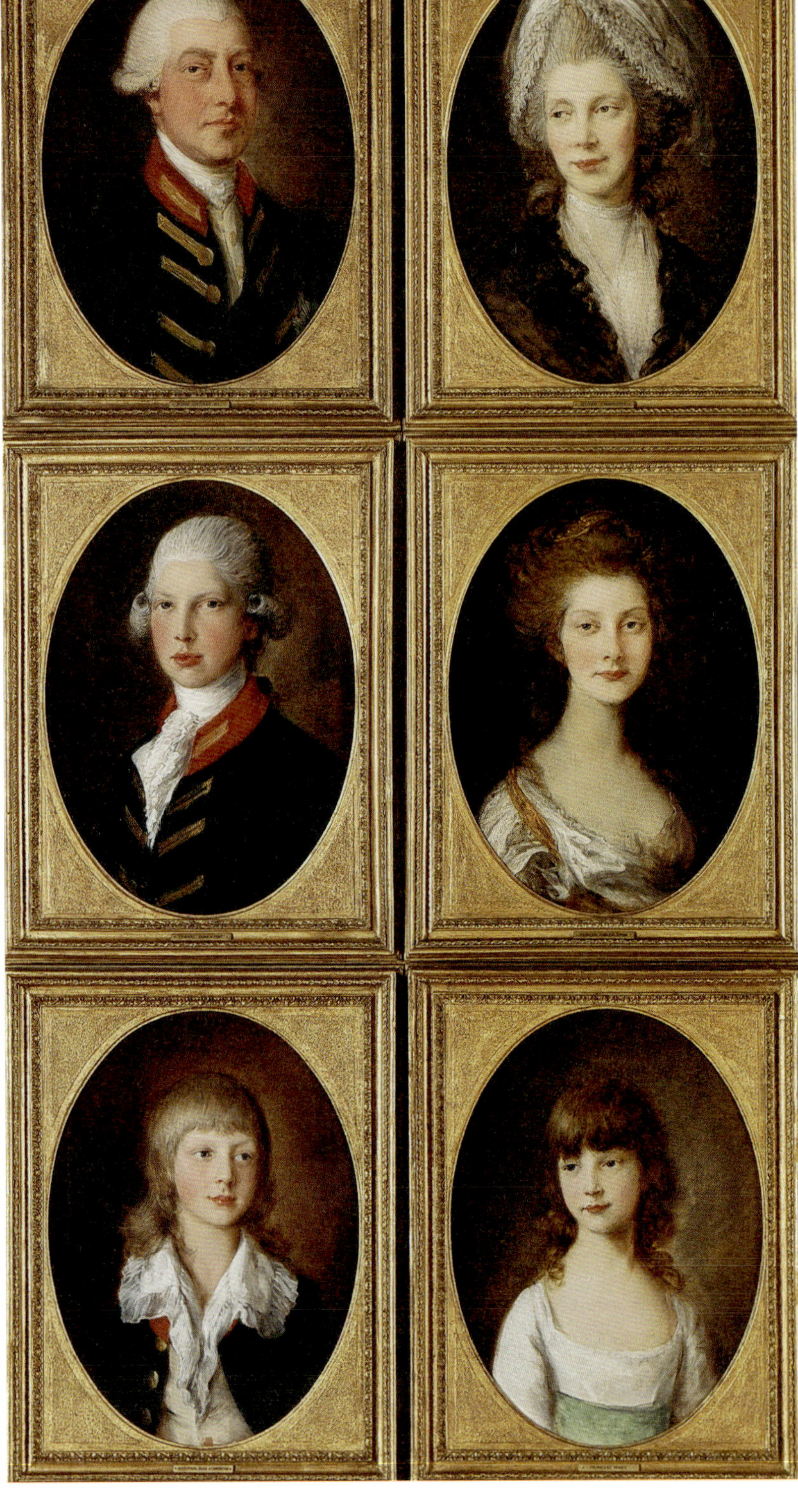

*Gainsborough's
Cottage Doors*

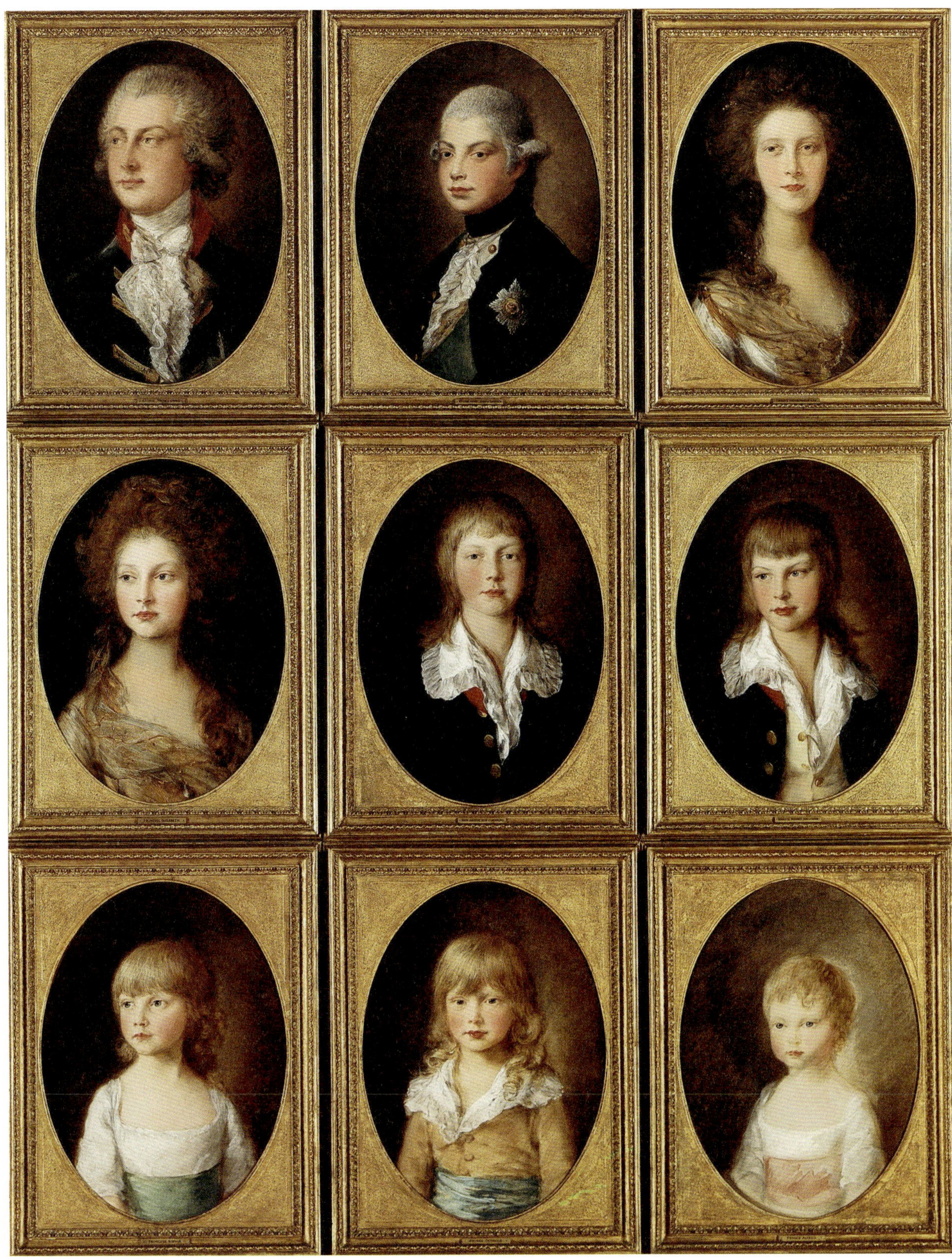

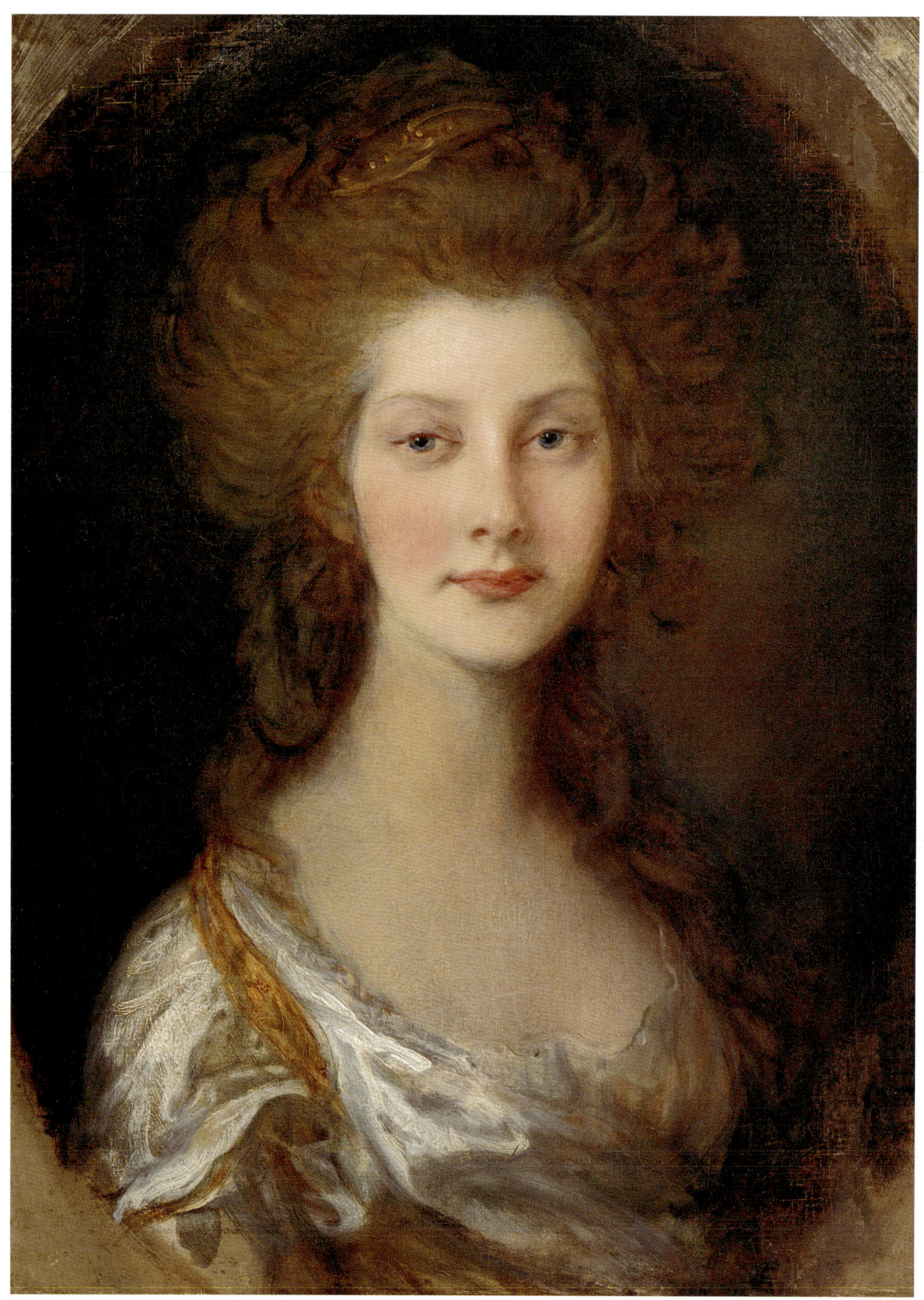

Detail of fig. 22, *Princess Augusta*

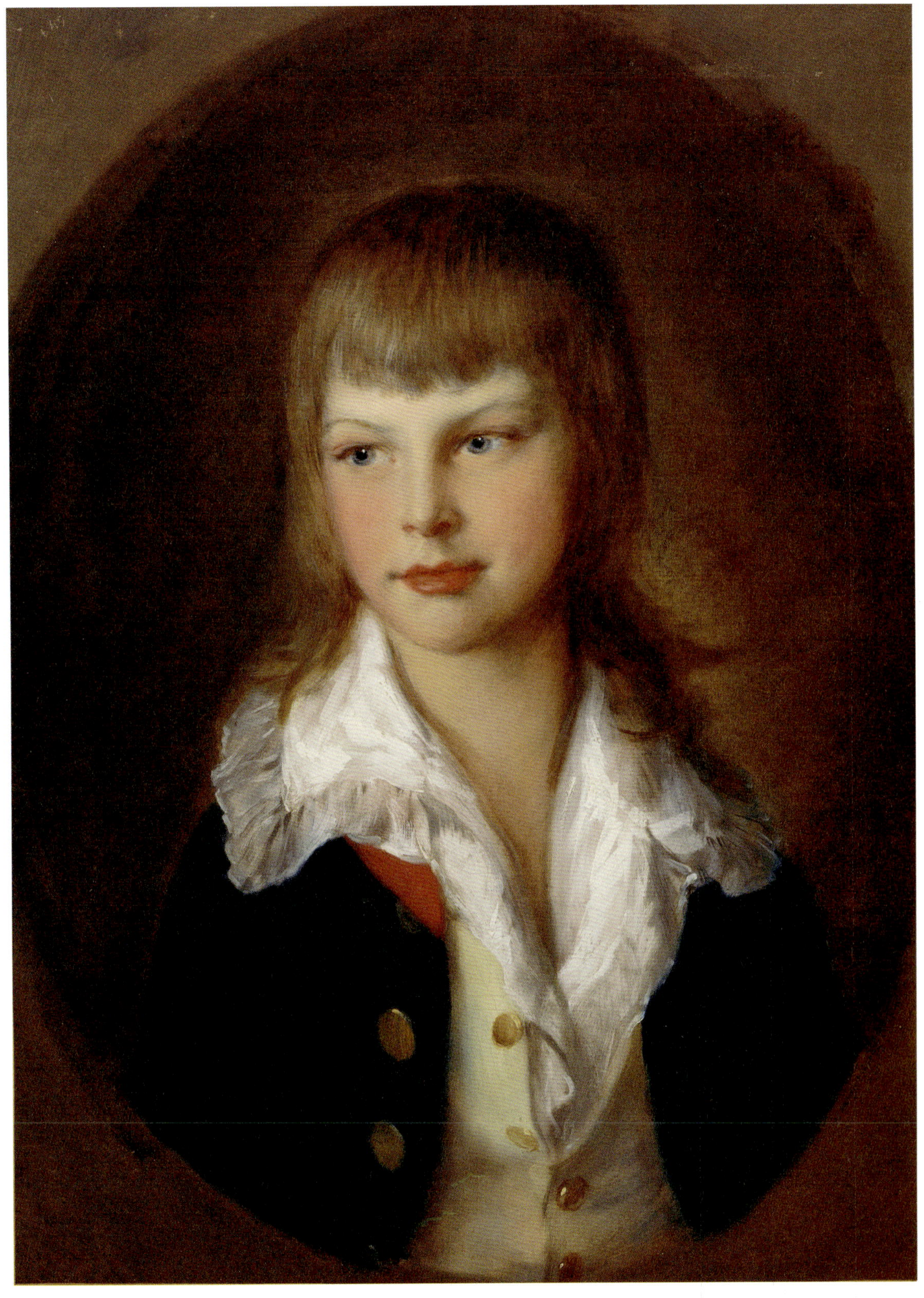

Detail of fig. 22, *Prince Augustus, later Duke of Sussex*

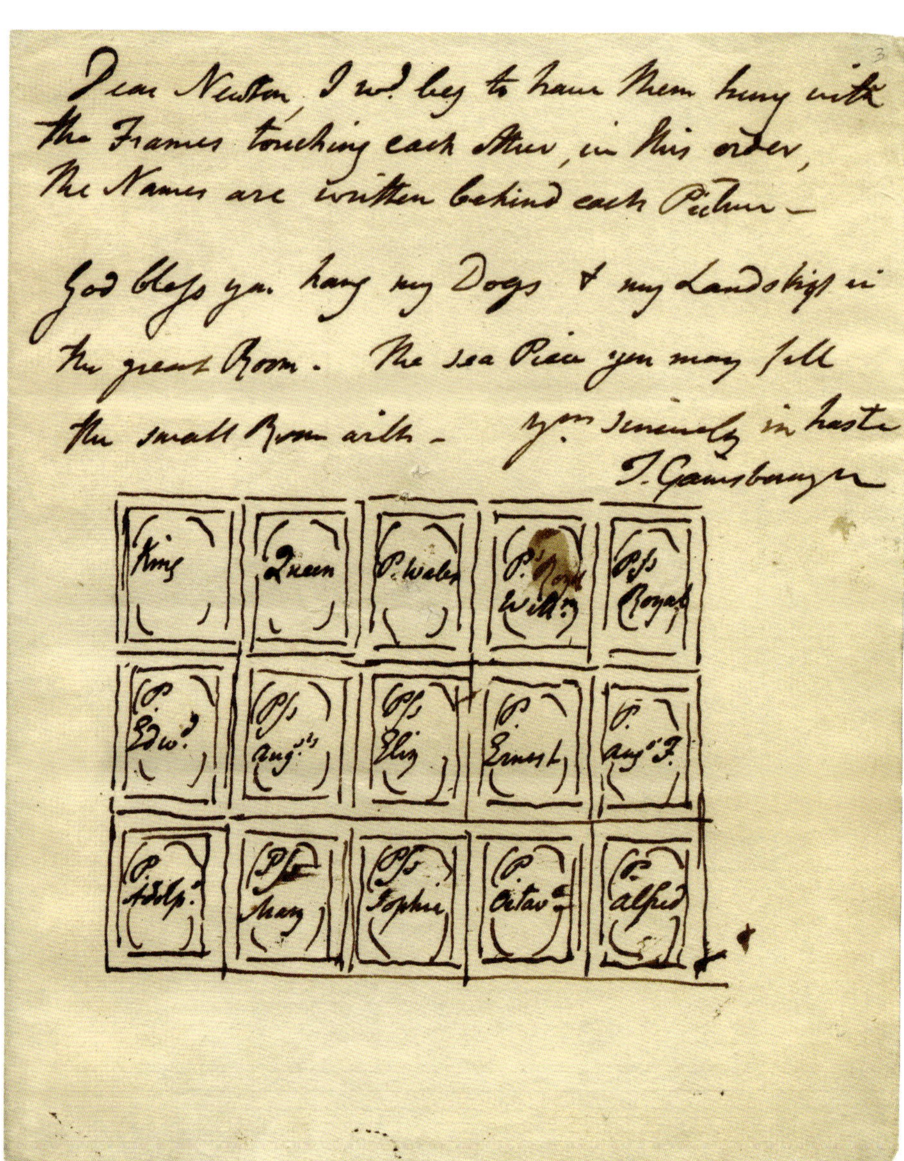

Gainsborough's
Cottage Doors

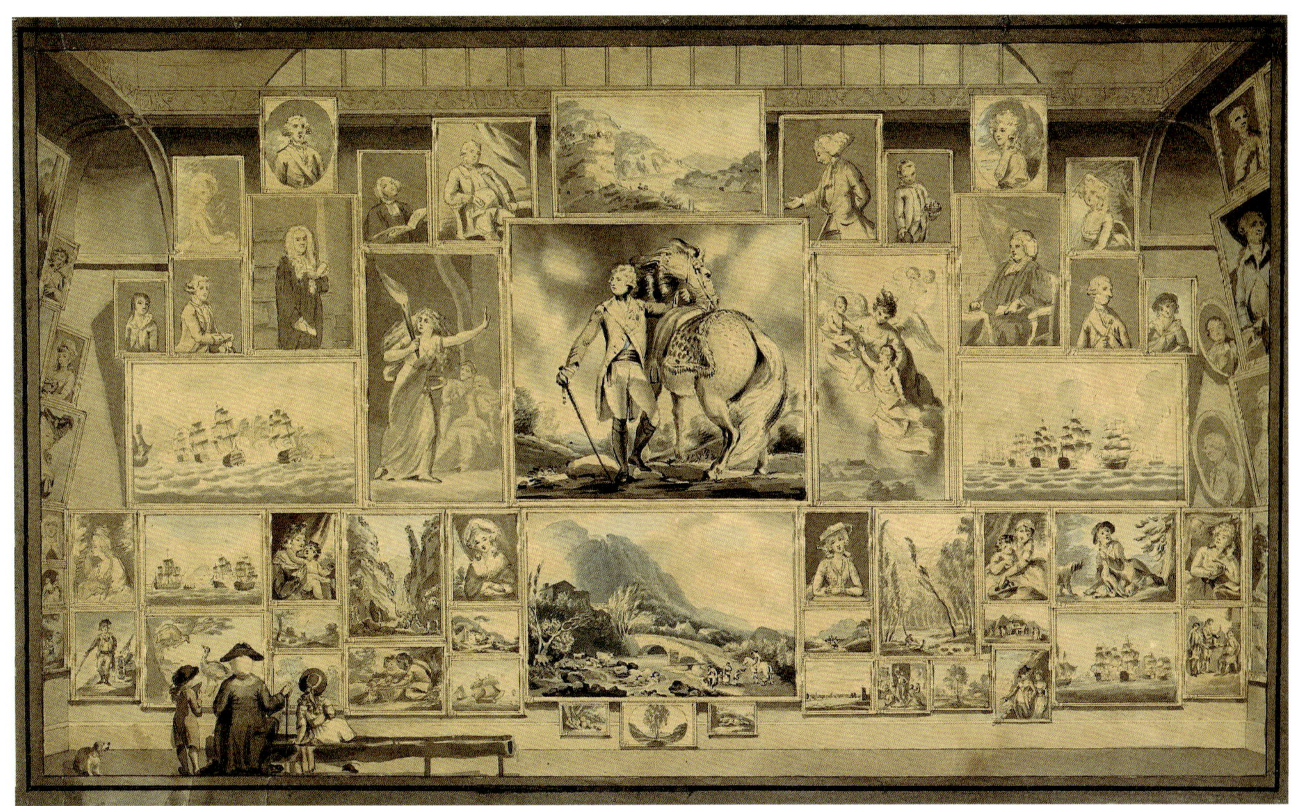

they formed an object large enough, in the Academy's view, to be
hung 'above the line'. When this was suggested Gainsborough
responded with a broadside, "Mr Gainsborough presents his
Compliments to The Gentlemen appointed to hang the Pictures
at the Royal Academy; and begs leave to *hint* to Them, that if The
Royal Family, which he has sent for Exhibition, *(being smaller than
three quarters)* are hung above the line along with full lengths, he
never more, whilst he breaths, will send another Picture to the
Exhibition – This he swears by God".[26] Gainsborough's arrogant

*Gainsborough's
Cottage Doors*

retort – at best an extraordinarily presumption – was clearly
bolstered by mixed feelings from the Academy, which did not
wish to offend their patron the king but yet did not feel it was
possible to accommodate Gainsborough's request. Sadly no
visual record of the hang is recorded but the portraits were
exhibited and so it must be presumed that the Academy
officials capitulated.

A recently discovered letter shows that Gainsborough
submitted his exhibits very late: "The Pictures shall all be sent
as fast as possible; you have all the Frames except the Duke
[of Northumberland]'s and your list is perfectly right – the two
¾ pictures are Lady Horatia Waldegrave, and Lord Cornwallis
– M[r] Ramus I sent yesterday".[27] The portrait of Lady Horatia
(fig. 25) arrived so late that it had to be mounted on the chimney
screen, which resulted in *The Gazetteer and New Daily Advertiser*
commenting on 23 May 1783, "The situation the *portrait* of *Lady
Horatia Waldegrave* has at the Royal Academy, it being hung
against the *chimney-board*, is sufficient to provoke the temper of
an Anchorite; and tho' every body must admit she would make
a charming companion for a *fire-side*, it is not necessary that she
should occupy the very *fire-place*; particularly while she has it in
her power to *kindle flames* by other means!"

There was another painting, overlooked in the correspondence,
that Gainsborough must have delivered to the Academy rather
earlier. *Girl feeding pigs* (fig. 26) is painted on two pieces of canvas
and may originally have been conceived as showing the doleful
girl alone; the pigs may well have been an afterthought. Another
contemporary reference tells us that three unruly piglets created
mayhem in the studio while the artist was painting them.
As the *Morning Herald* (1 May 1782) records, the painting was
"… a great favourite with the public, and justly so: the little

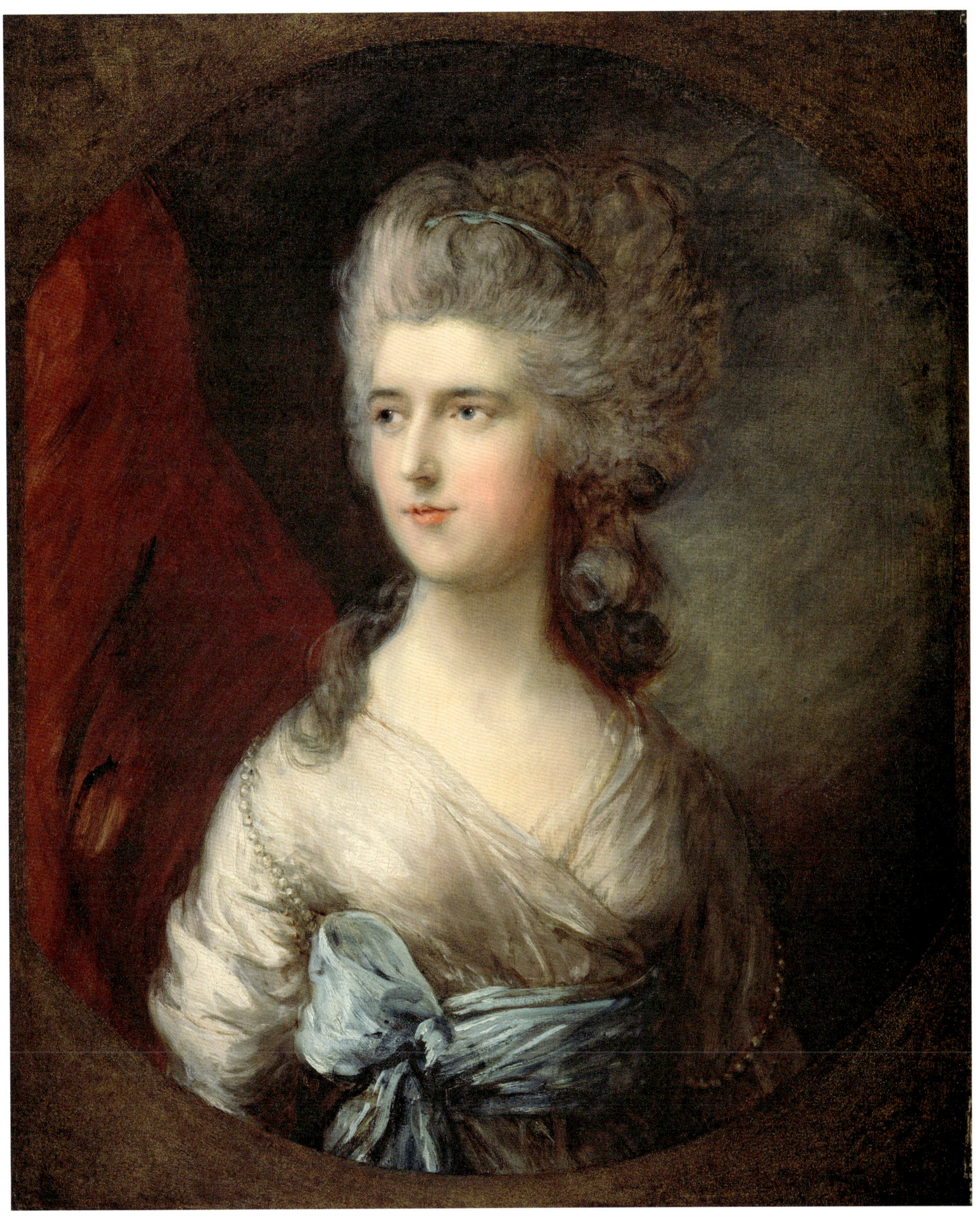

FIG. 26
Thomas Gainsborough
Girl feeding pigs, 1781–82
Oil on canvas, 125.7 × 148.6 cm
Castle Howard collection, York

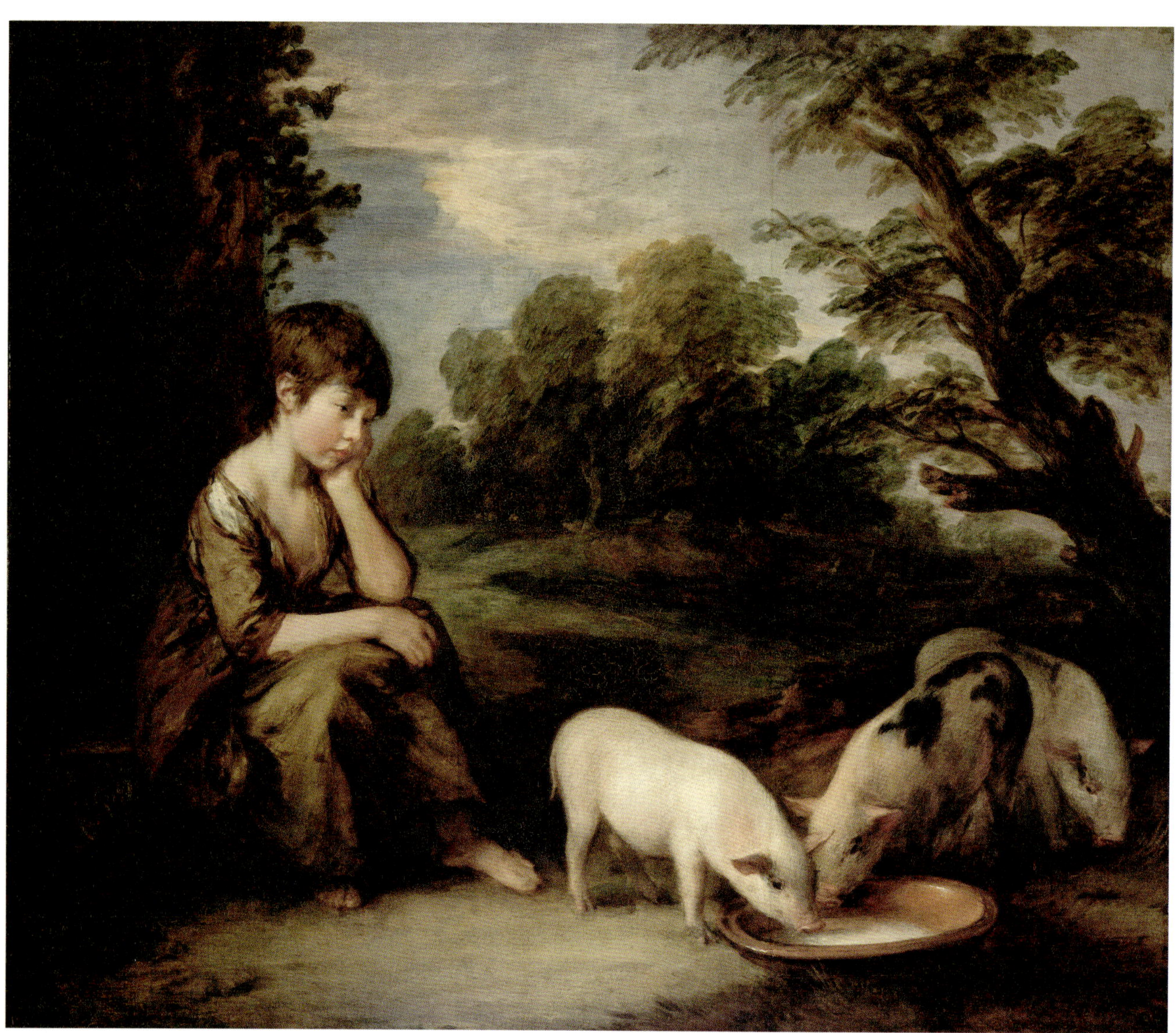

pigs are inimitably executed, and the girl is exquisitely painted". Reynolds, no doubt conscious of the tension between Gainsborough and the Academy's hanging committee, attempted to curry favour with his rival and bought the painting for the princely sum of £200. Reynolds's response prompted a gracious and light-hearted letter from Gainsborough, "I think myself highly honour'd, & much Obliged to you for this singular mark of your favour; I may truly say that I have brought my Piggs to a fine market".[28] Perhaps conscious that he might further offend Gainsborough in his next Discourse, which he would deliver in December, Reynolds made two appointments with "Mr Gainsborough", on Sunday 3 November and Sunday 10 November. James Northcote, Reynolds's pupil, states that Gainsborough had invited his rival to sit for a portrait, which was aborted as Reynolds was taken ill; however, it seems likely that this was a front for airing the two artists' differences and prompted by a bid by the President to keep Gainsborough within the Academy's fold.[29]

There is a marked disparity between Gainsborough's abrupt correspondence with the Academy's hanging committee and a rather more friendly letter to the Academy's Treasurer, Sir William Chambers. Gainsborough first remarks about his own, "cunning way of avoiding great subjects in painting …", then adds, with a degree of false modesty, that "if I can do this while I pick pockets in the portrait way two or three years longer I intend to sneak into a cot & turn a serious fellow; but for the present I must affect a little madness. I know you think me right as a whole, & can look down upon Cock Sparrows as a great man ought to do with compassion."[30] The antagonism between artist and institution was now entrenched and it was reprised the following year.

FIG. 27
Thomas Gainsborough
The Three Eldest Princesses
Oil on canvas, cut down to
129.5 × 179.9 cm
Royal Collection

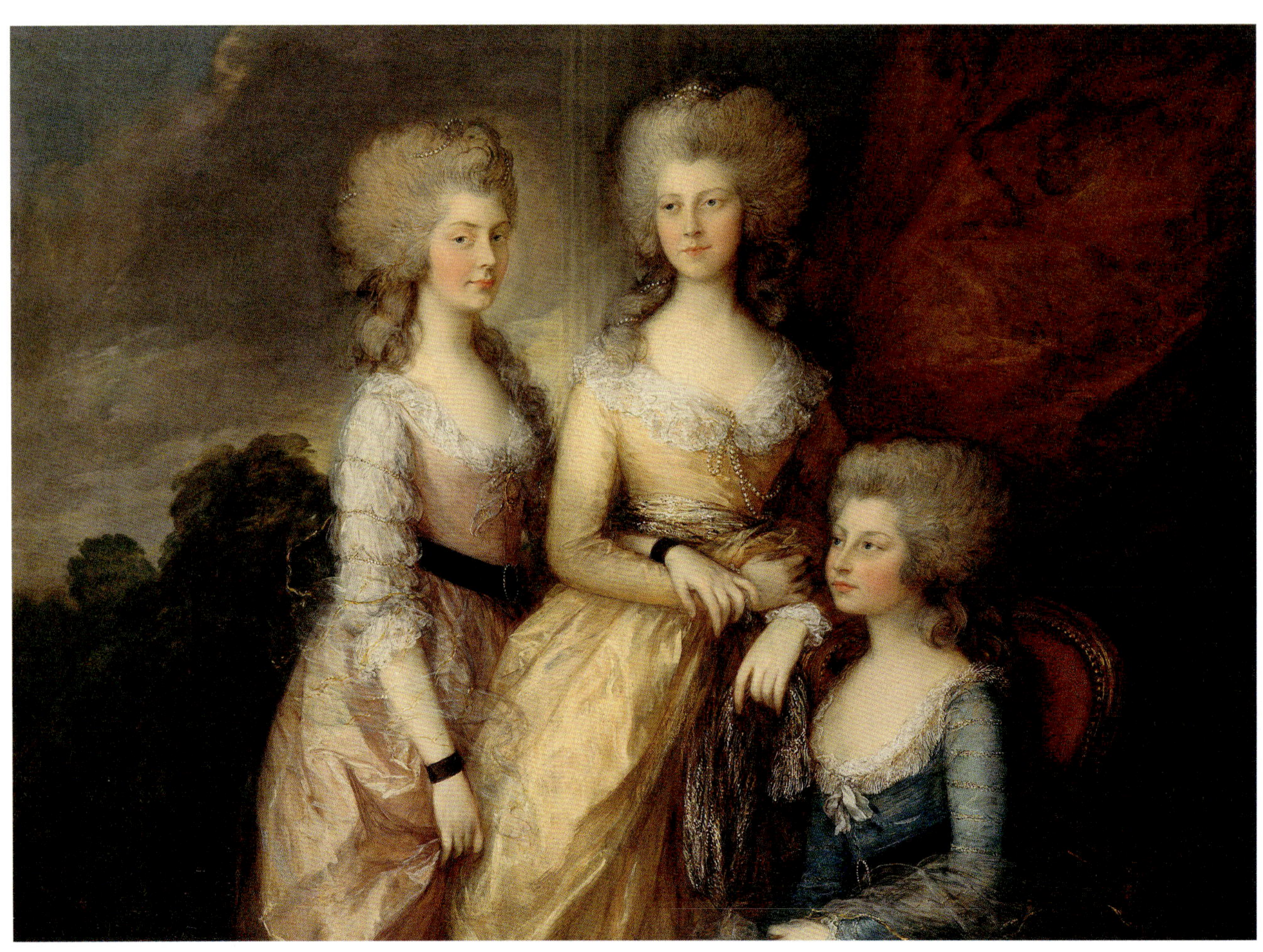

In the spring of 1784 Gainsborough completed a triple
portrait of the three eldest daughters of George III, a canvas that
had been commissioned by the Prince of Wales for the Saloon
at Carlton House (figs. 27 and 28). The painting remained in
Gainsborough's studio until the decoration of the Saloon was
finished. Dorothy Richardson saw the picture in Schomberg
House on 7 March 1785, when she described the sitters as
"the Three Eldest Princesses, two standing, & one sat they look
handsome chearful, fat Women".[31] The design of the room had
been well advanced when Gainsborough received the commission
and, most importantly, the height at which the paintings were to
hang had been dictated when the portrait was first discussed, and
Gainsborough had duly accommodated these requirements in
his design.

The triple portrait was destined for the exhibition at the
Academy and was included amongst a series of thumbnail
sketches illustrating all his intended submissions in a letter to
the Academy (fig. 29). On this occasion, perhaps in feigned
cooperation, Gainsborough provided sketches rather than the
frames. It was an ambitious submission, including six full-lengths
and two group portraits, and the list may well have included some
canvases that had not even been started. The sketch of William
and Edward Tomkinson included a dog that was omitted from
the final composition and the double portrait, now in the Taft
Museum, Cincinnati, may in fact not have been painted until the
following winter. Similarly there is some evidence to suggest that
the portrait of Lord Hastings was only begun in earnest in May,
and payment was only forthcoming in the following August.[32]
If this was the case, while Gainsborough was clearly keen to
show the committee the works they might anticipate receiving,
his action also demonstrated that he was confident that the

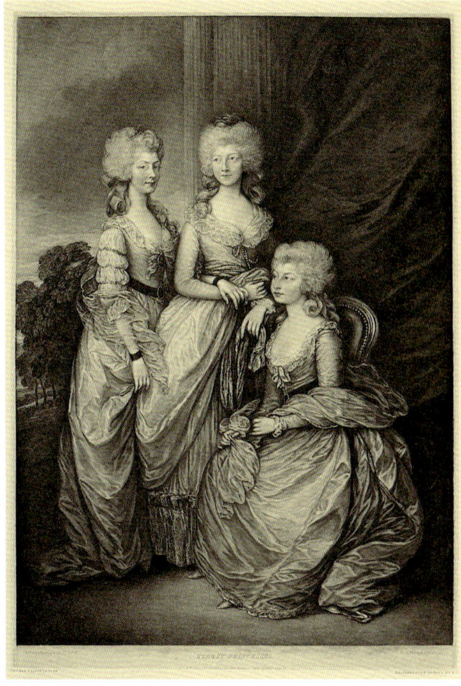

FIG. 28
Gainsborough Dupont
after Thomas Gainsborough
The Three Eldest Princesses, 1793
Mezzotint, 655 × 454 mm
British Museum, London

FIG. 29
Enclosure with Gainsborough's letter
to the Royal Academy, [April] 1784
Royal Academy of Arts, London

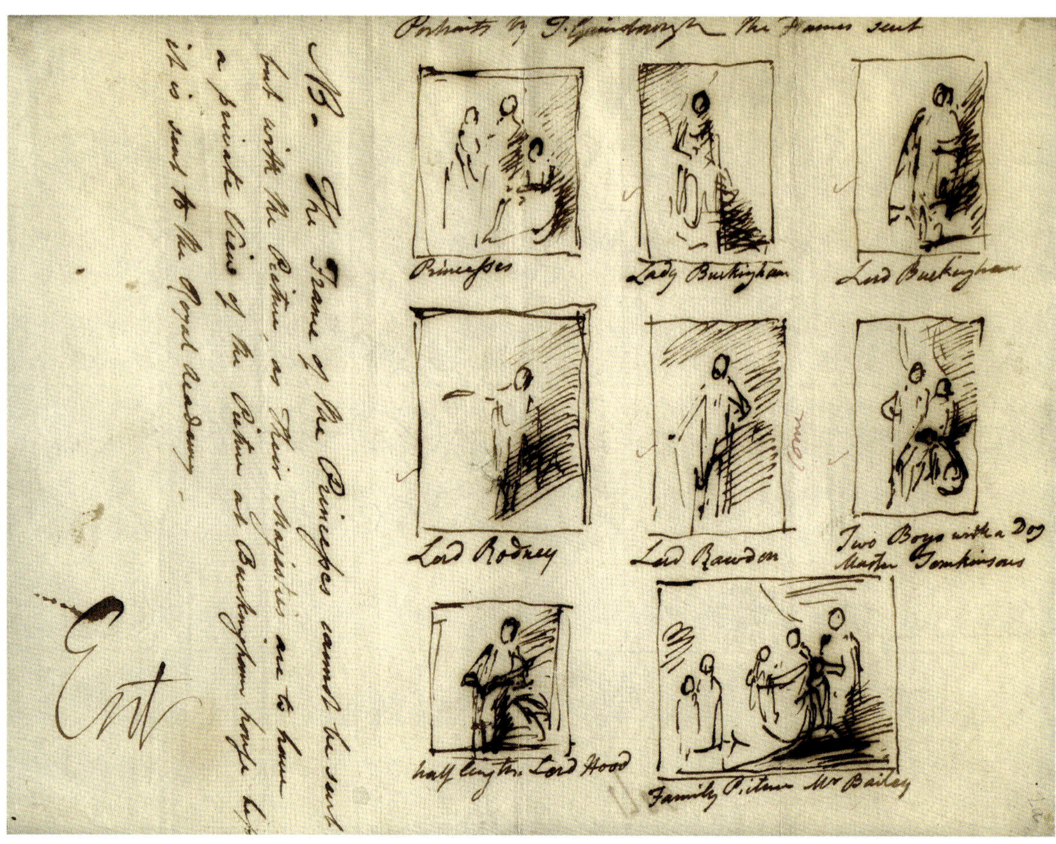

Gainsborough's
Cottage Doors

Academy's committee would behave in a predictable way and
not call his bluff.

Gainsborough demanded that the bottom of the portrait of the
Eldest Princesses should be placed no more than five feet six inches
from the floor. The portrait was eight foot or so in height so if
it were hung at that height the canvas would cover 'the line' and
destroy the tried and tested hang of the exhibition. Gainsborough
had made the Hanging Committee a totally unreasonable request
and, once it was rejected, he withdrew all his paintings from the
exhibition.

On 26 April 1784, the *Morning Post and Advertiser* reported
the story:

> The public have to regret the umbrage which Mr.
> Gainsborough has taken at the conduct of the Council at
> Somerset-House, as it will most probably suppress the public
> Exhibition of the works of that eminent artist at any place;
> he sent six whole length pictures subject to the disposition
> of the gentlemen who are appointed to arrange the different
> productions, with information at the same time, that he was
> painting another canvas to contain whole-lengths of the
> Princess Royal, Princess Augusta, and Princess Elizabeth,
> observing also, that he should finish it in a stile which would
> not appear to advantage at a greater height than five feet six
> inches, and therefore he desired to be indulged with such a
> situation, though it might interfere with the general rule,
> otherwise he would not have his picture exposed. To this
> he was respectfully answered, that a compliance with his
> request would break through an established plan, and derange
> the whole exhibition; therefore hoped he would submit the
> disposition of his intended picture to the principles of society.

The *Whitehall Evening Post*, reporting on 22 April 1784, suggests that the Academy had tried to accommodate Gainsborough's testing requests: "He sent word that pictures of such and such specific dimensions would come from him; he at the same time directed that they should all have such and such particular situations in the rooms. These directions were in part offered to be complied with. Entirely to follow them was impossible. This being communicated to Mr. Gainsborough he returned a very laconic note that the Exhibition should have none of his pictures."

Three months later, when the dust had begun to settle, Bate in the *Morning Herald* on 26 July 1784 was able to take up the artist's cause:

> The illiberality with which Mr. *Gainsborough's* Pictures were treated by the *Counsel* who regulate the hanging of the *Pieces* exhibited at the *Royal Academy*, was such, that consistent with his own consequence and honor, he was under the necessity of withdrawing them from the *Academy*, previous to the late exhibition. They are however of a nature too important to the improvement of science, not to merit public attention.

The journalist continues with a description of the triple portrait of the princesses:

> The limbs and other parts are *rounded* sweetly and delightfully to the eye; but from there being calculated for tender effect, should not be surveyed at a great distance. The figures are connected with the utmost harmony and skill, and the drapery finished very highly. Neither strong masses of *light* nor *shade* are to be observed in the *composition*, and of course the transitions are the gentler and more agreeable. The back ground is formed of drapery, and a landscape, enriched with a beautiful sky.

Gainsborough had removed himself from the Academy and had cast off the shackles of producing paintings, competitive in their design and colouring, which constrained the artist's natural goals of likeness, subtlety and balanced tonality. He could now be choosey about the commissions he accepted, paint for his own pleasure and satisfy his own curiosity.

Notes

1 John Hayes, *The Letters of Thomas Gainsborough*, New Haven and London 2001, p. 116.

2 See Susan Sloman, 'Gainsborough and "the lodging-house way"', *Gainsborough's House Review*, 1992–93, pp. 23ff.

3 Philip McEvansoneya, 'An Irish Artist Goes to Bath: Letters from John Warren to Andrew Caldwell, 1776–1784', *Irish Architectural and Decorative Studies*, II, 1999, p. 165.

4 "Tea drinkings …" comes from Gainsborough's letter to William Jackson dated Bath 4 June: Hayes 2001, p. 68. Wright's letter dated Bath 9 February 1776 is quoted by William Bemrose, *The Life and Works of Joseph Wright, A.R.A. …*, London 1885, p. 45.

5 Susan Sloman, 'Gainsborough in Bath 1758–59', *Burlington Magazine*, CXXXVII, August 1995, pp. 509–12, and Michael Rosenthal, 'Testing the Water: Gainsborough in Bath in 1758', *Apollo*, CXLII, September 1995, pp. 49–54.

6 Gainsborough thought his illness was due to "a single trip I made in London … and occasioned by the uncertainty which followed the foolish Act": Hayes 2001, p. 22. He was tended by Drs Charleton and Moysey and notice of his death was printed (prematurely) in the *Bath Journal* on 17 October and corrected in the subsequent issue a week later: W.T. Whitley, *Gainsborough*, London 1915, p. 43.

7 Gainsborough's letter of resignation is dated 5 December 1768: Hayes 2001, p. 62.

8 Hayes 2001, pp. 112–13.

9 E.K. Waterhouse, *Gainsborough*, London 1958, p. 82, no. 504.

10 The arrangements are detailed in John Pye, *Patronage of British Art, An Historical Sketch*, London 1845, pp. 123–24.

11 Waterhouse 1958, p. 62, no. 179.

12 Lesley Lewis, 'Elizabeth, Countess of Home, and Her House in Portman Square', *Burlington Magazine*, CIX, August 1967, pp. 443–53.

13 Oliver Millar *et al.*, *Van Dyck: A Complete Catalogue of the Paintings*, New Haven and London 2004, pp. 488–89, no. IV.75 repr.

14 John Hayes, *The Landscapes of Thomas Gainsborough*, 2 vols., London 1982, pp. 434–36, nos. 92 and 93 repr.

15 Larissa Dukelskaya and Andrew Moore, *A Capital Collection: Houghton Hall and The Hermitage*, New Haven and London 2002, pp. 216–17 repr. col.

16 Friday, 28 April 1775, p. 2.

17 Thursday, 27 April 1775, p. 2.

18 Walpole's comment appears in his annotated copy of the exhibition
   catalogue (Earl of Rosebery collection).

19 *Morning Herald*, 1 May 1781.

20 Viola Pemberton-Piggott cleaned the painting before it was included in
   the exhibition at Tate Britain in 2002. I am grateful to her for sharing her
   thoughts on this painting.

21 John Hayes, *Gainsborough as Printmaker*, London 1971, p. 17, figs. 54, 59
   and 64.

22 Michael Rosenthal, *The Art of Thomas Gainsborough: A little business for the Eye*,
   New Haven and London 1999, pp. 257–62.

23 The sentiment was repeated in *The Morning Chronicle*, 1 May 1781, p. 3.

24 Hayes 2001, p. 148.

25 In the less dense hangs of earlier exhibitions, the final "handsome frames"
   were used, as Gainsbrough mentions in a letter to Lord Aldborough dated
   21 March 1771: Hayes 2001, p. 83.

26 Hayes 2001, p. 150.

27 The letter is in the Royal Academy library. I am grateful to Stephen Pomeroy
   for bringing this letter to my attention.

28 Hayes 2001, p. 147.

29 The appointments are listed in Reynolds's Sitter's Book for 1782 (Royal
   Academy, London) and Northcote's comments appear in *Conversations of
   James Northcote R.A. with James Ward*, ed. Ernest Fletcher, London 1901,
   p. 159.

30 The letter is dated 27 April 1783: Hayes 2001, p. 152.

31 Hugh Belsey, 'Some Artists' Studios Described in 1785', in *Windows on that
   World: Essays on British Art Presented to Brian Allen*, privately printed, London
   2012, p. 126.

32 Details which lead to these conclusions are given in the author's forthcoming
   catalogue raisonné of portraits by Gainsborough.

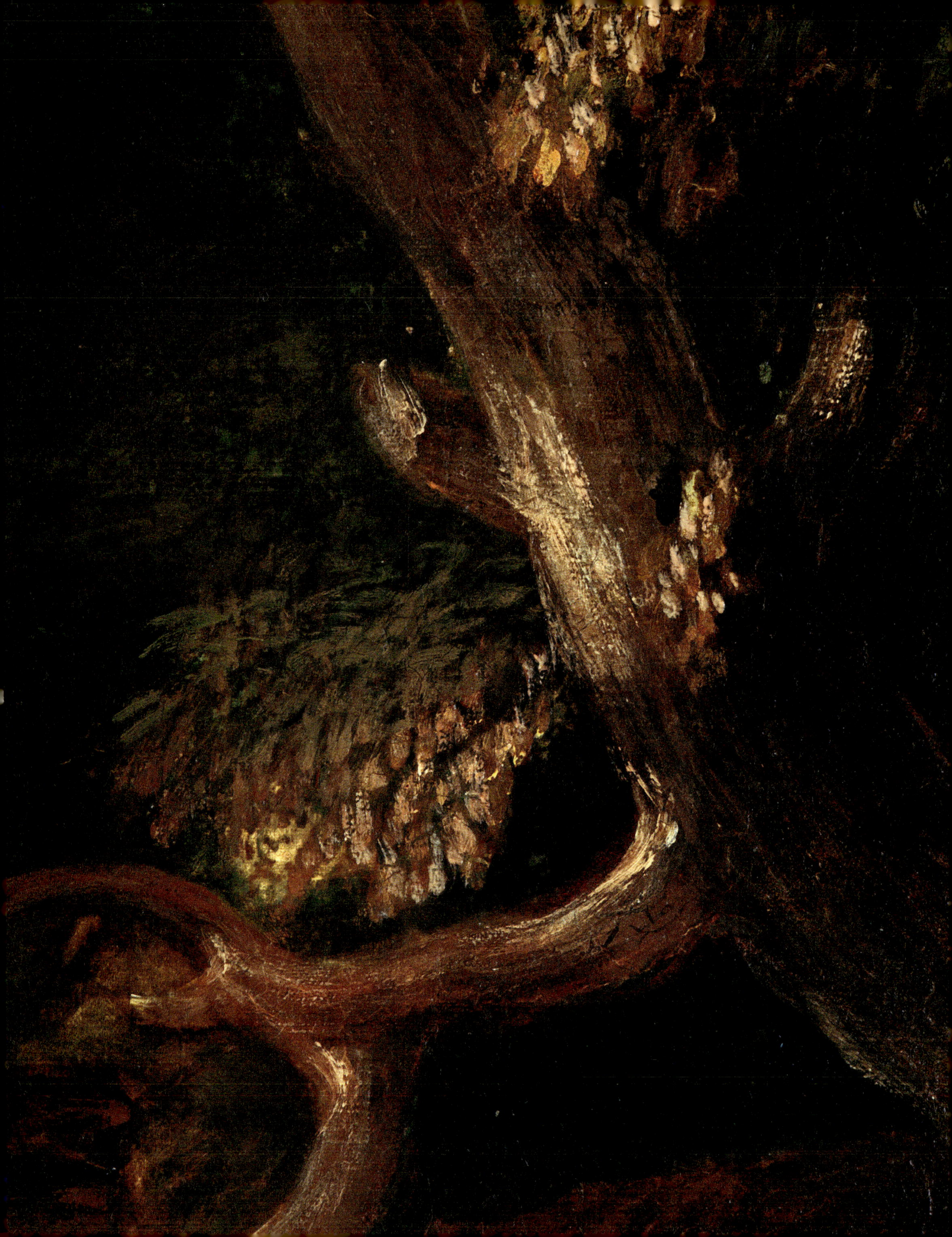

"The whole force of his genius"

AFTER GAINSBOROUGH HAD MANUFACTURED HIS EXIT
from the Academy, the pace of his work changed. It was more
relaxed and more considered and, to some extent, his output
reflected his own interests rather than those of his clients.
A slower pace gave him the opportunity to reflect and to make
adjustments to his paintings. His so-called 'fancy' pictures took
up more of his energies; he spent longer painting some full-
length portraits, while others appear to be dashed off; in pose his
head-and-shoulder portraits became more formulaic and there
was an added emphasis on painting landscape. There had been
intimations of all these changes in his work for three or four years
but by removing himself from the Academy he had gained greater
independence and freedom and so was able to direct his energies
to areas of work on which he wished to concentrate.

Gainsborough's reputation for 'fancy' pictures had been
established with the exhibition of *A shepherd* at the Academy in
1780. *Girl feeding pigs* was exhibited at the Academy in 1782 and his
rival Sir Joshua Reynolds purchased it, though the motives behind
the purchase, probably multifarious, are unknown. To ensure the
popularity of the paintings Gainsborough had commissioned
the Irish engraver Richard Earlom to scrape mezzotints of both;
judging from the number of prints known today, *A shepherd*
found a better market. Other canvases were produced soon
after: *Two shepherd boys and fighting dogs* (The Iveagh Bequest,
Kenwood) was exhibited at the Academy in 1783 and, searching
around the studio, Gainsborough found an unfinished double
portrait of Elizabeth and Thomas Linley that he had started to
paint in Bath nearly twenty years earlier: he cut it down, added
some lightening streaks of paint that turned the costume into
rags and sold it as a 'fancy' picture together with commissioned
portraits and two landscapes to the Duke of Dorset in 1784, a

FIG. 30
Thomas Gainsborough
Beggar boy and girl (adapted
from a portrait of Elizabeth and
Thomas Linley), 1768 and 1784
Oil on canvas, 69.8 × 62.3 cm
Sterling and Francine Clark Art
Institute, Williamstown

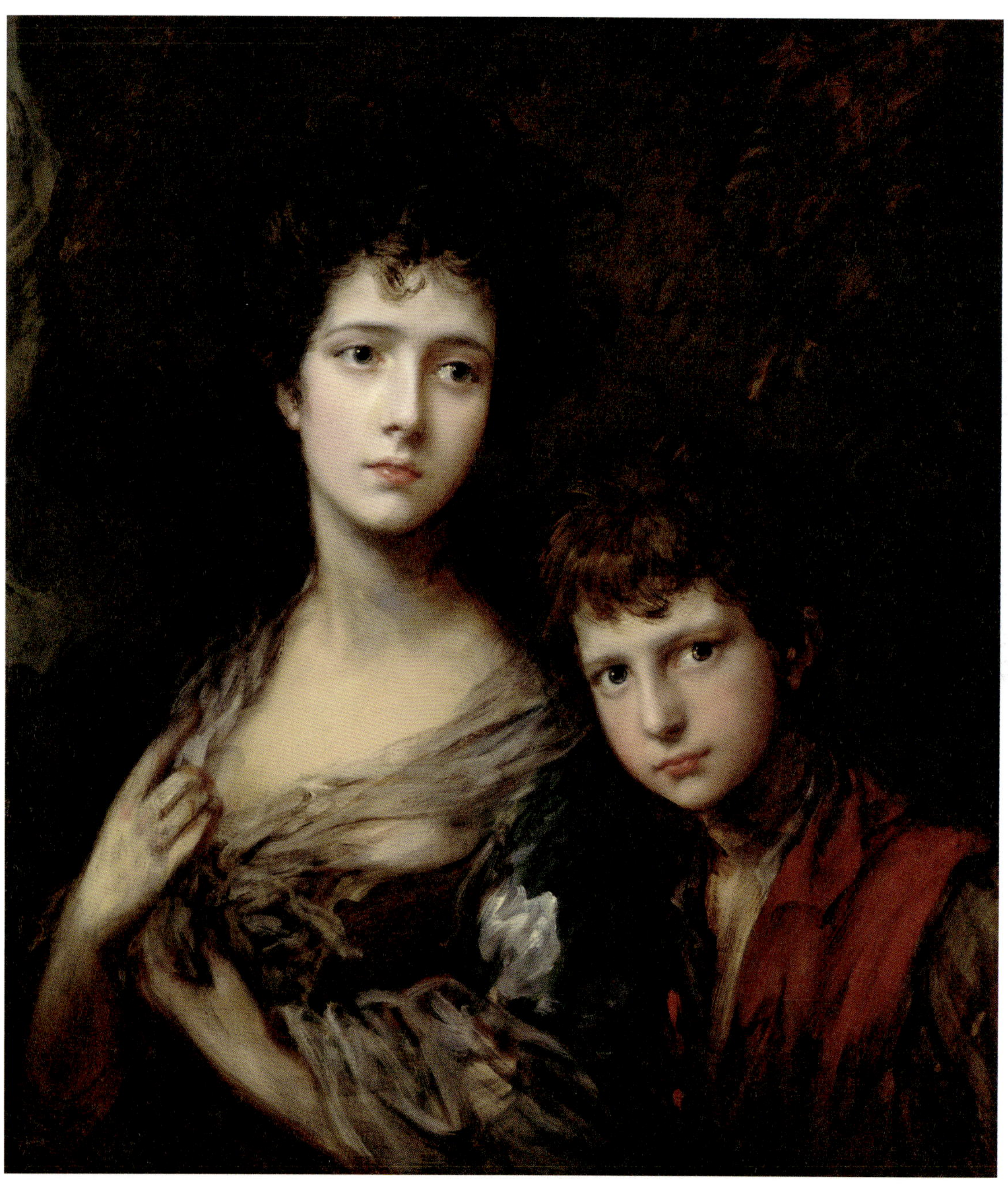

sale that is recorded in a receipt for £105 (fig. 30).[1] Later 'fancy'
pictures consisted, for example, of a single figure posing with a
puppy and a broken jug, holding a bowl of milk or accompanied
by a cat, or of two vulnerable children riding an ass, gathering
wood, or eating gruel beside a fire. All these subjects provided
the basis for Gainsborough's later reputation and after his death
their exhibition encouraged engravings to be made of them by
speculative engravers.

During the 1780s a number of youthful sitters visited
Schomberg House. Young politicians, often with radical views,
seem to have favoured Gainsborough's approach to portraiture.
He generally painted the head within a feigned oval on a rectan-
gular canvas, which he presented in a standard oblong frame
with a slip decorated with olive sprigs or some other motif in the
spandrels (fig. 31). The arrangement gave the portraits a greater
intimacy and placed more emphasis on the head, and it built on
the artist's strong reputation for catching a likeness. As the artist
had stated so unequivocally fifteen years earlier, likeness was "the
principal beauty & intention of a Portrait".[2]

Gainsborough became increasingly uneasy painting full-
length portraits during this period. The size of the canvas the
format dictated, approximately sixty inches wide – the standard
width of a loom – and between ninety and ninety-five inches high,
required something more than a single figure to fill it. It is worth
noting that two portraits painted for exhibition in his studio in
1760 and 1770 respectively avoided the constraints consequent
upon a commission: those of Mrs Thicknesse (Cincinnati Art
Museum) and the 'Blue Boy' (The Huntington, San Marino), are
painted on much smaller canvases. John Hayes has already noted
the banal rhetoric of the portraits of the Hon. George Cranfield
Berkeley and of Sir Peter Burrell (fig. 32),[3] but the portrait of Lord

FIG. 31
Thomas Gainsborough
William Pearce, c. 1783
Oil on canvas, 71.1 × 60.3 cm
Private collection, London

The portrait is shown in its original frame.

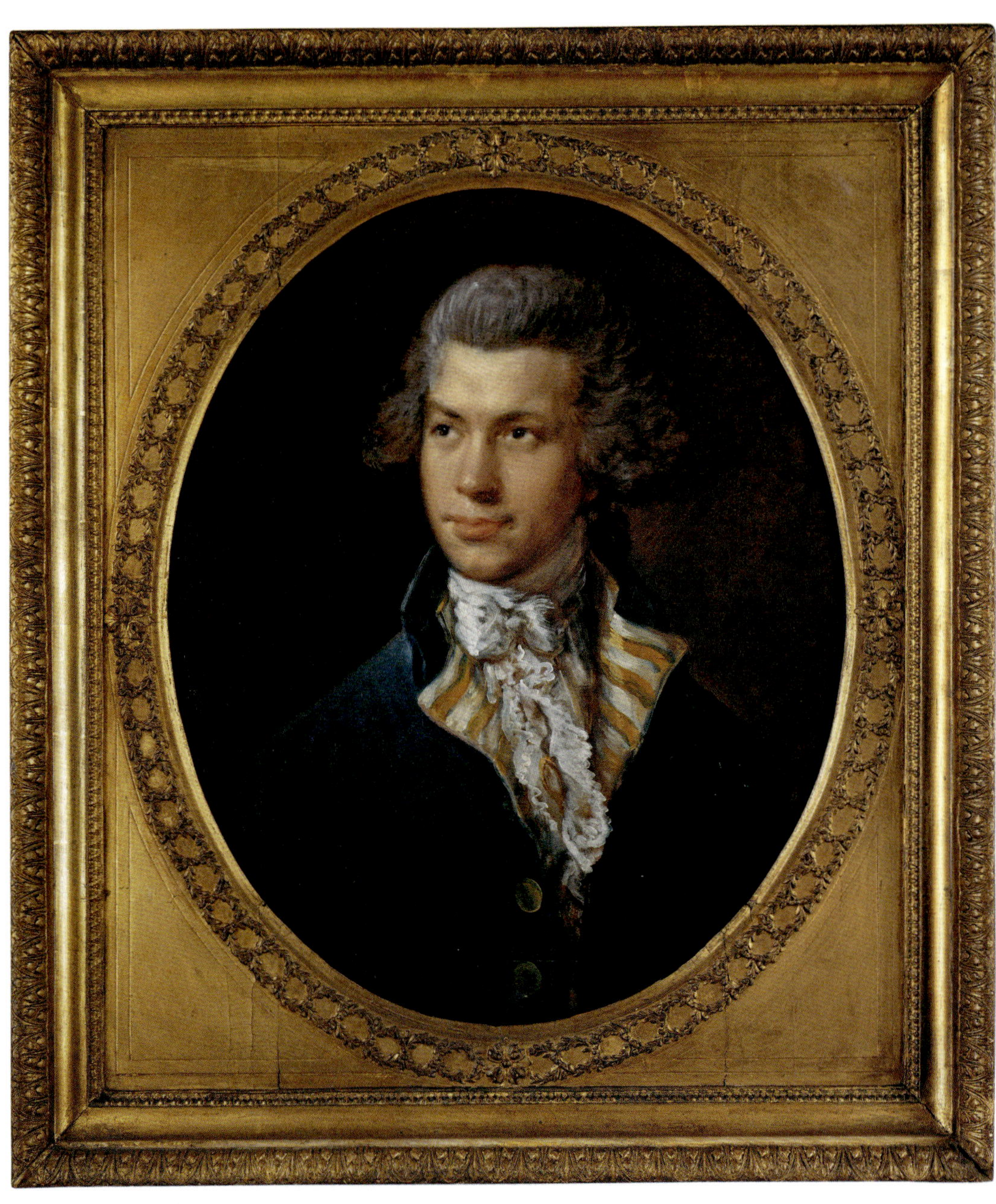

FIG. 32
Thomas Gainsborough
Sir Peter Burrell, later Lord Gwydir, 1787
Oil on canvas, 248.9 × 184.2 cm
Newport Restoration Foundation,
Rough Point, Newport

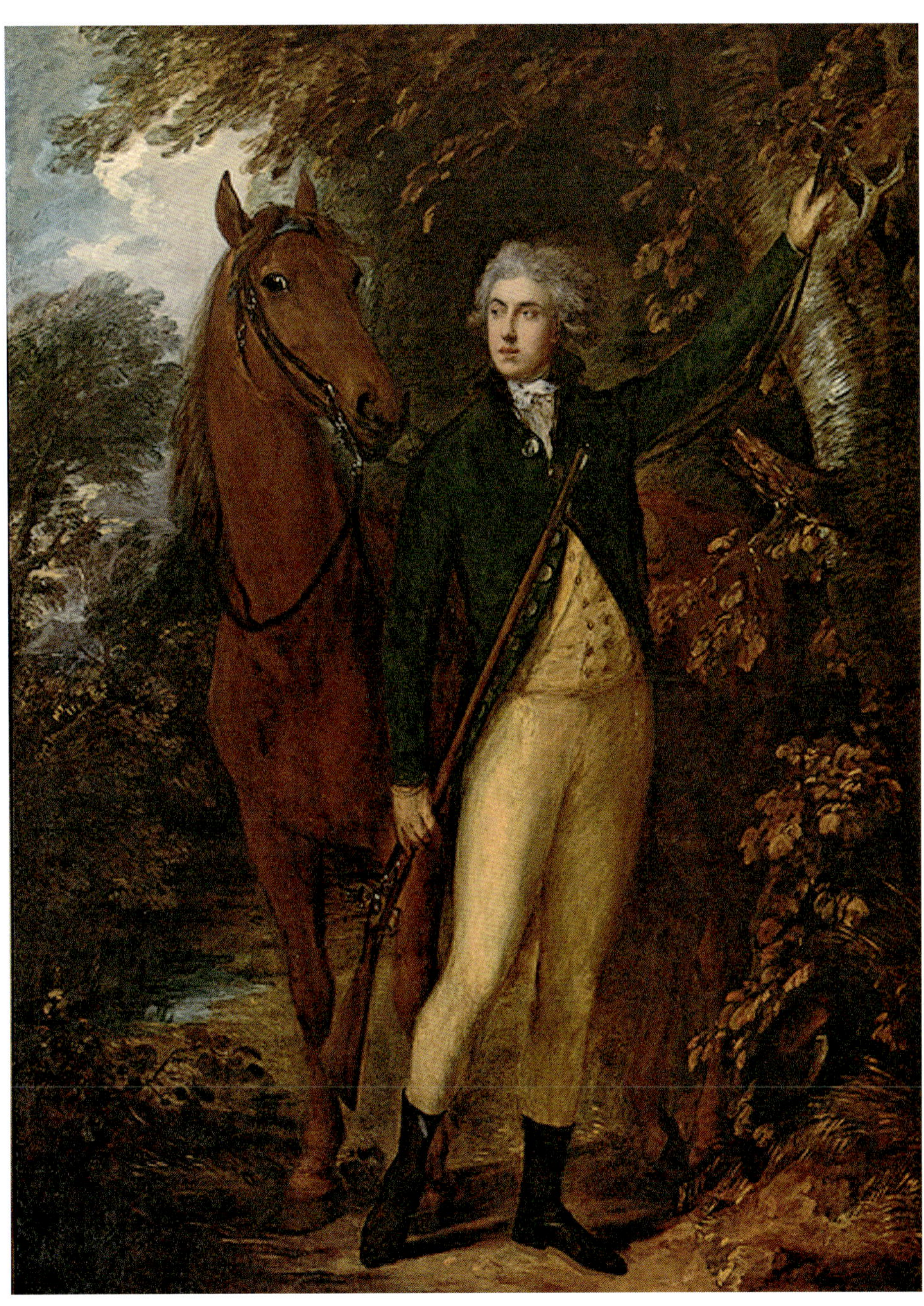

Gainsborough's
Cottage Doors

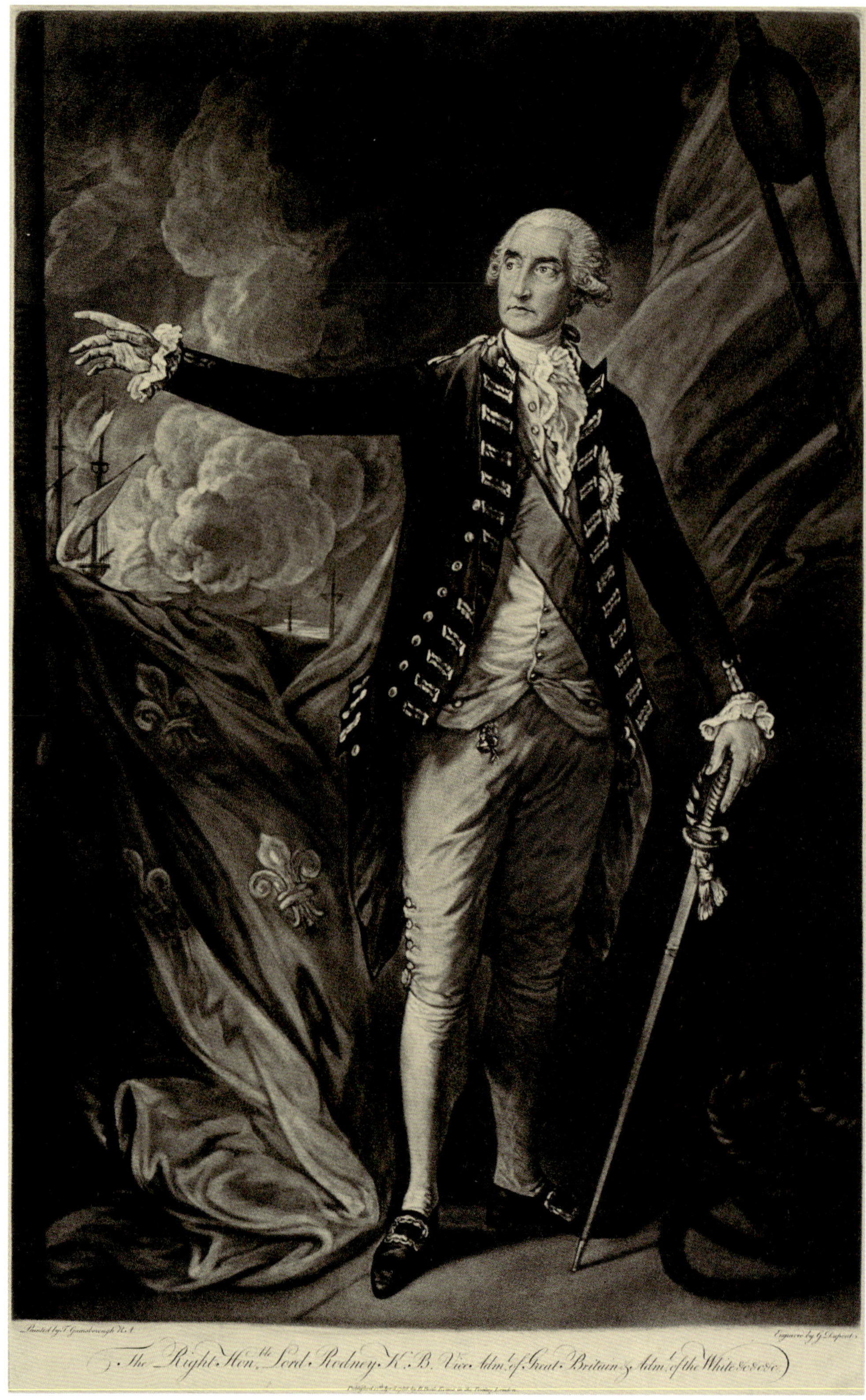

Rodney, painted for Berrington Hall in Herefordshire for his important patron Thomas Harley (one of Harley's daughters had married the sitter's son), manages the pose more comfortably. In the canvas Rodney is shown on the quarter-deck of the *Formidable* commanding the British Navy against the French in the Battle of the Saints, which resulted in a victory that ensured Britain maintained control of Jamaica. According to one press report there were plans for the sitter to be accompanied by a bantam cock as one had "continued crowing from the beginning to the end of the action of the 12th of April [1782]".[4] There is no trace of the bird in the final canvas and, if it were ever included, Gainsborough presumably removed it realising that a cockerel would have done little to add to the *gravitas* of the piece. The portrait was clearly a success as a mezzotint was commissioned from Gainsborough's assistant Gainsborough Dupont and published on 12 April 1788 (fig. 33).

Other portraits of the 1780s were extensively revised in the studio. By contrast to the portrait of Rodney, Gainsborough seems have been more engaged in painting the portraits of the Rt Hon. Charles Wolfran Cornwall (fig. 34), Mrs Sheridan (fig. 35) and 'Perdita' Robinson, and he used costume, landscape and sometimes a dog to overcome the problem of filling a standard-sized full-length canvas. Recent conservation treatment and X-ray photography of the portraits of Mrs Sheridan (fig. 36) and Mrs Robinson (Wallace Collection, London) have shown that both canvases were subjected to great change and that they were clearly the subject of concentrated rethinking and reappraisal. Mrs Sheridan was originally shown as a shepherdess, then her attributes were removed to make the canvas a straightforward, if somewhat idealized, portrait. A strip of canvas was removed from the left-hand side of the painting of Mrs Robinson and

*Gainsborough's
Cottage Doors*

replaced by another strip on the right-hand side of the painting to accommodate the dog.[5] Such radical changes show a certain indecisiveness, perhaps even a lack of confidence, and when Gainsborough was faced with a particular compositional problem he returned to his mentor, Sir Anthony van Dyck.

In 1772 William, 5th Earl of Essex presented a covered cup to his agent and "sincere friend" Thomas Clutterbuck (fig. 37). Ten years later Gainsborough was commissioned to paint a portrait showing the Earl seated confronting the beholder with Clutterbuck standing beside him holding the silver cup and pointing out the inscription with the index finger of his right hand. Gainsborough was uniquely able to express the differing situations of the two sitters, the confident Earl contrasted with the diffident servant, but the equal importance given to each figure presented a thorny compositional problem. It was solved when the artist looked at examples of double portraits produced by Van Dyck during his years in London. The recently authenticated portrait of the Cheeke sisters, Essex, Countess of Manchester and Lady Anne Rich, are a good example of the format which provided Gainsborough with a rubric for his design (fig. 38).

On Saturday 8 April 1786 the Henry Bate reported in the *Morning Herald* that "Mr. *Gainsborough* has of late been exercising his science upon some of those objects in rustic nature, on which the attention dwells with the fondest pleasure. He has produced seven imaginary views, the materials of which are in the utmost harmony of composition, and possessed of the highest torches [*sic*; touches?] of genius." All the landscapes he describes are small-scale and must have been painted as experiments to satisfy his personal interpretation of "harmony of composition". Several small landscapes have been associated with Bate's description, and they include a lyrical landscape now in the Chazen Museum of

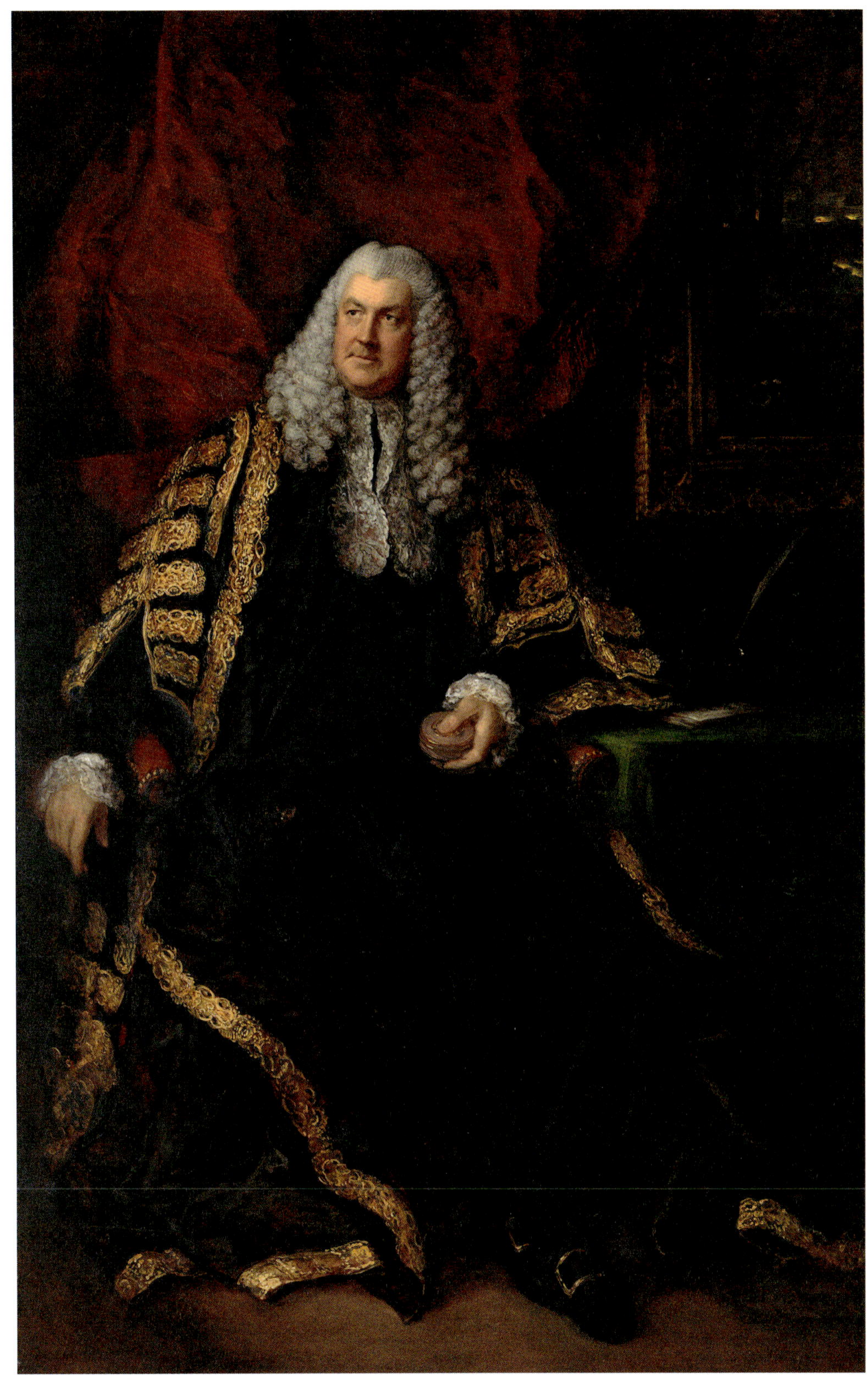

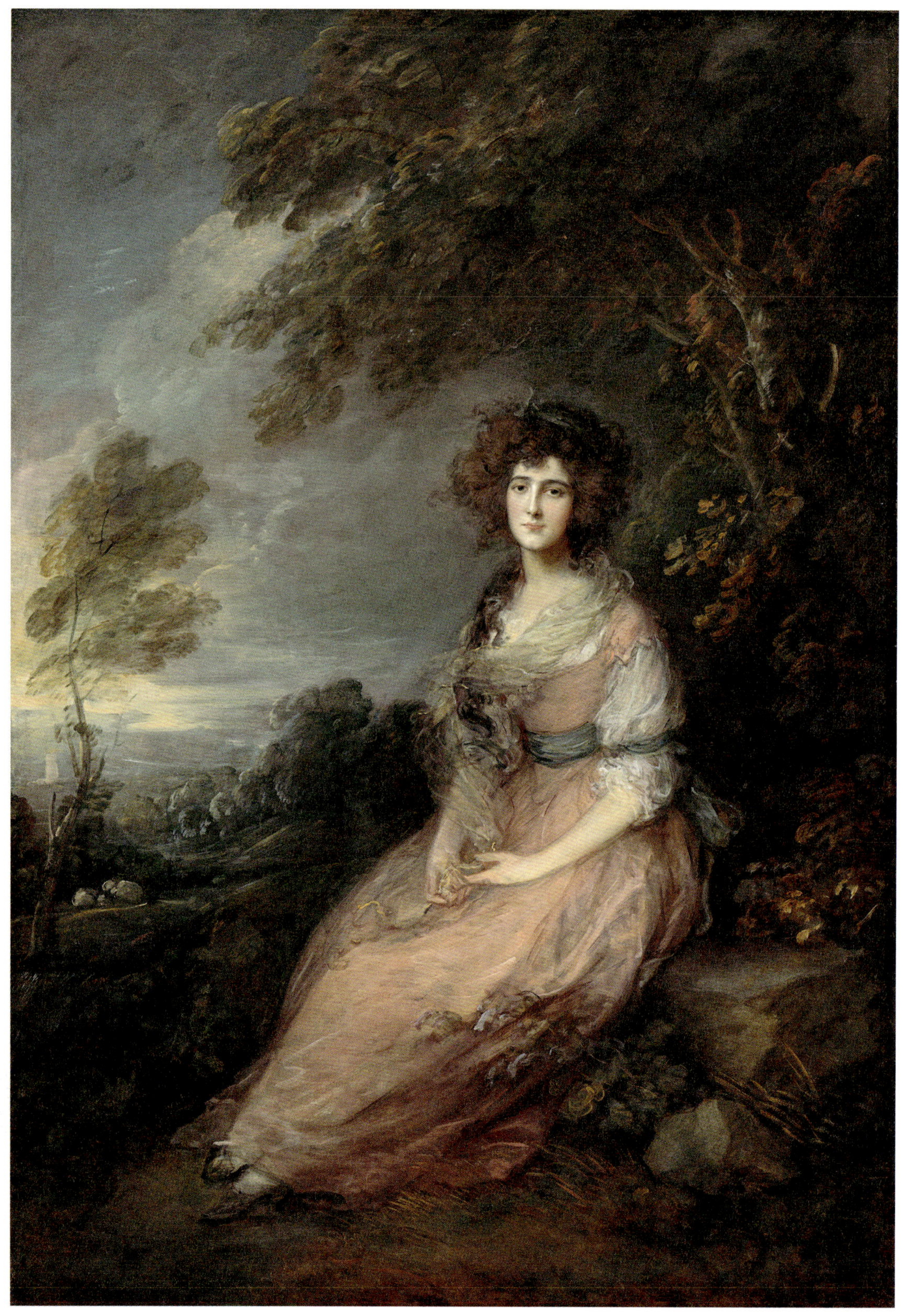

FIG. 35
Thomas Gainsborough
Mrs Richard Brinsley Sheridan, 1785–87
Oil on canvas, 219.7 × 153.7 cm
National Gallery of Art, Washington

FIG. 36
X-ray of *Mrs Richard Brinsley Sheridan*

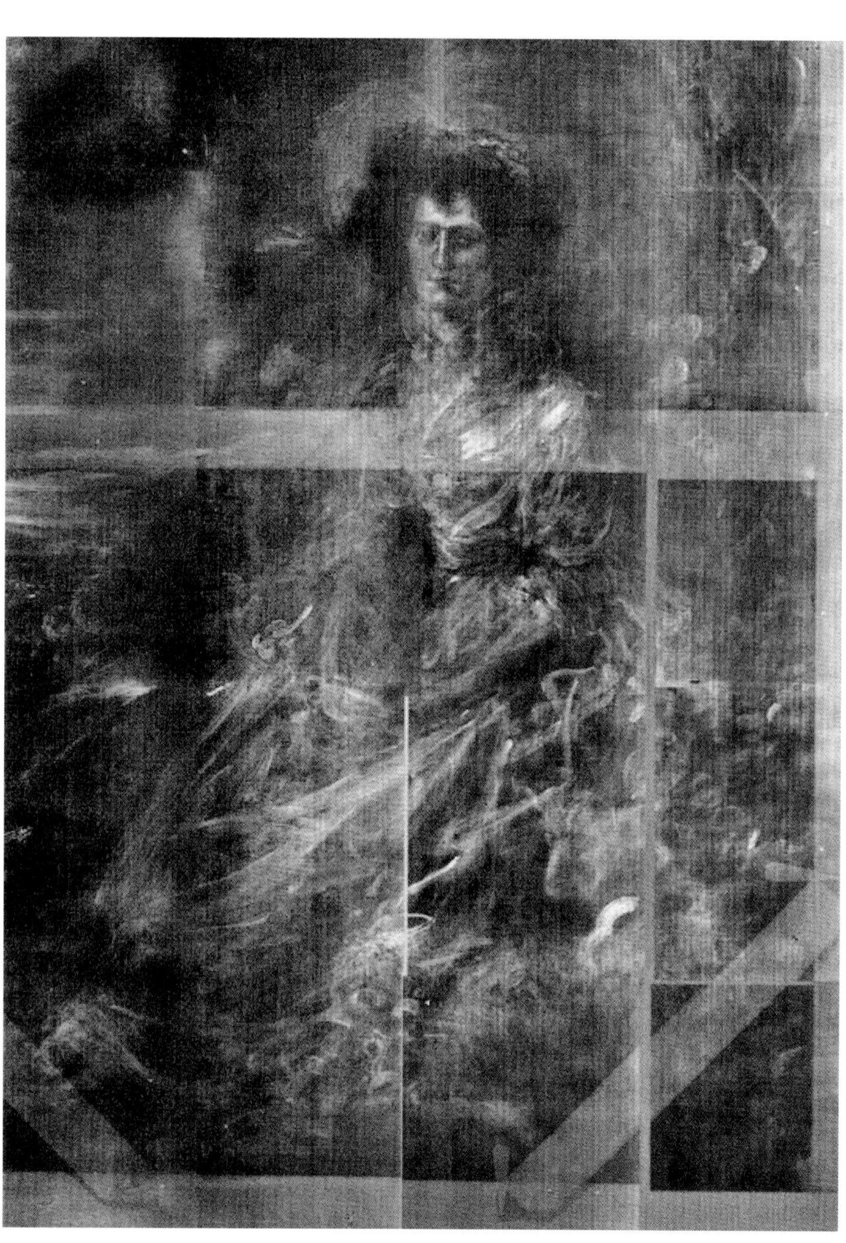

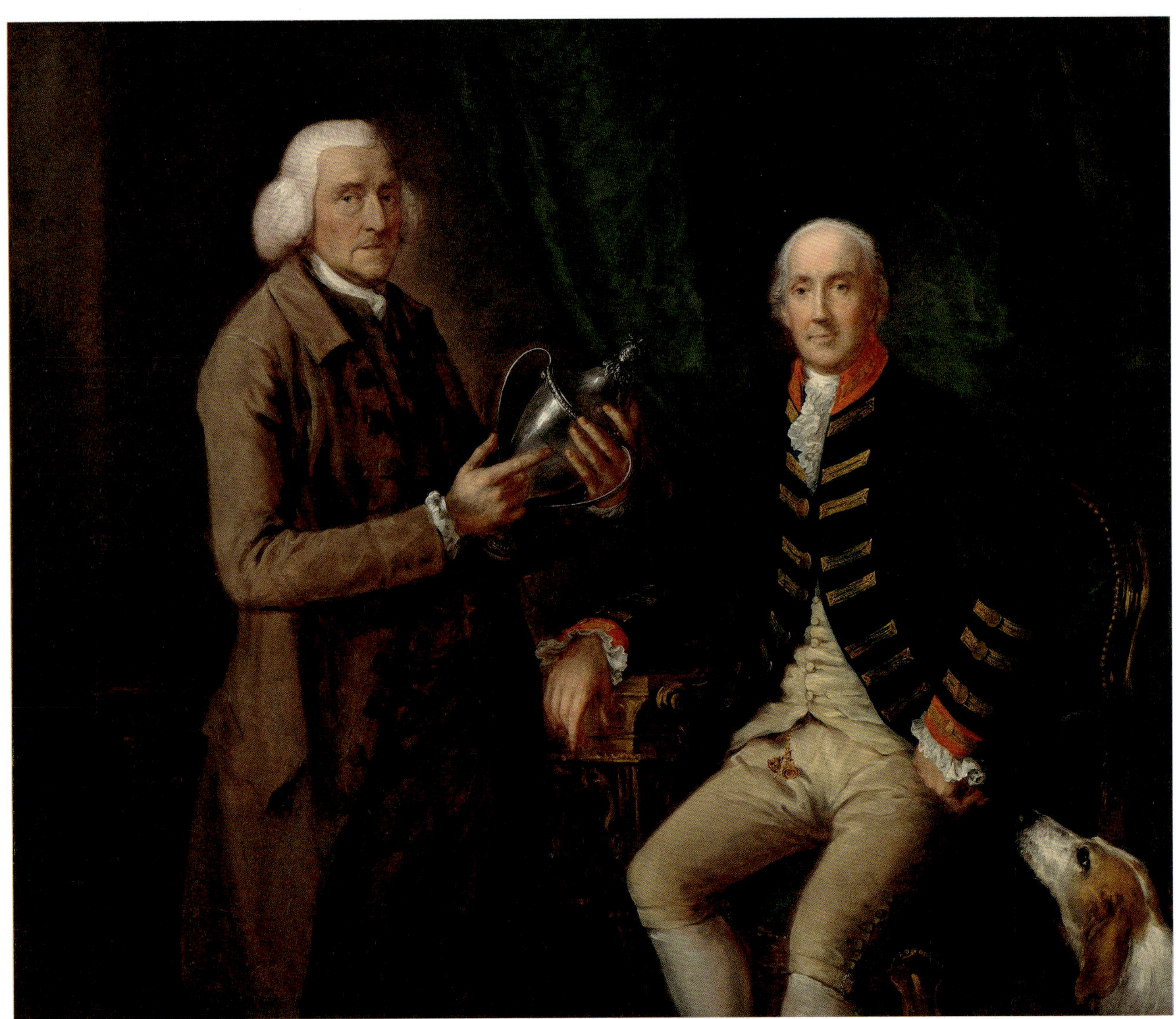

FIG. 37
Thomas Gainsborough
*William Anne Hollis Capell, 4th Earl
of Essex presenting a cup to Thomas
Clutterbuck*, before 1784
Oil on canvas, 148.5 × 174 cm
J. Paul Getty Museum, Los Angeles

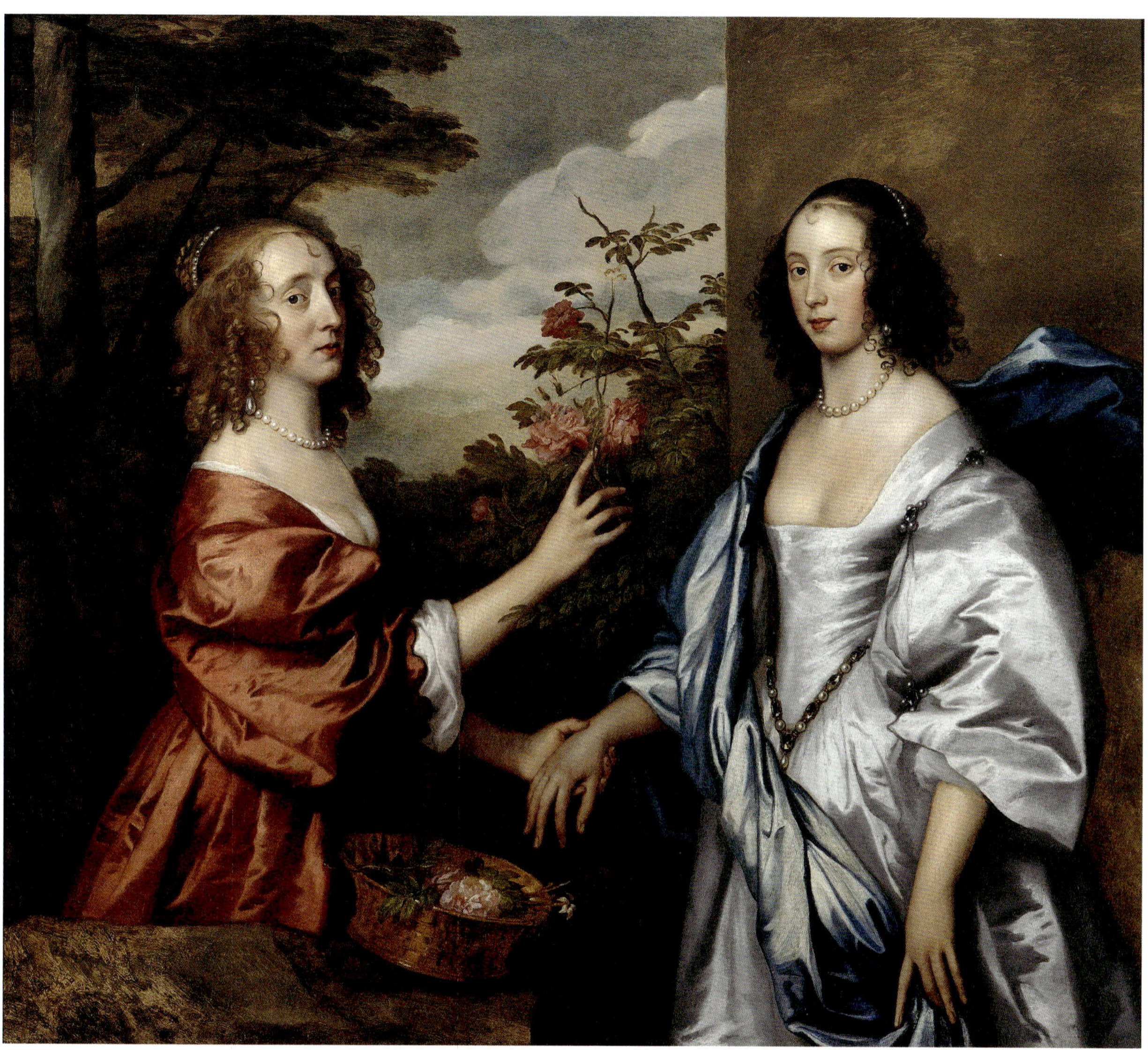

FIG. 38
Anthony van Dyck
*Essex, Countess of Manchester and Lady
Anne Rich (The Cheeke Sisters), c.* 1640
Oil on canvas, 130.8 × 1490.2 cm
Private collection, Los Angeles

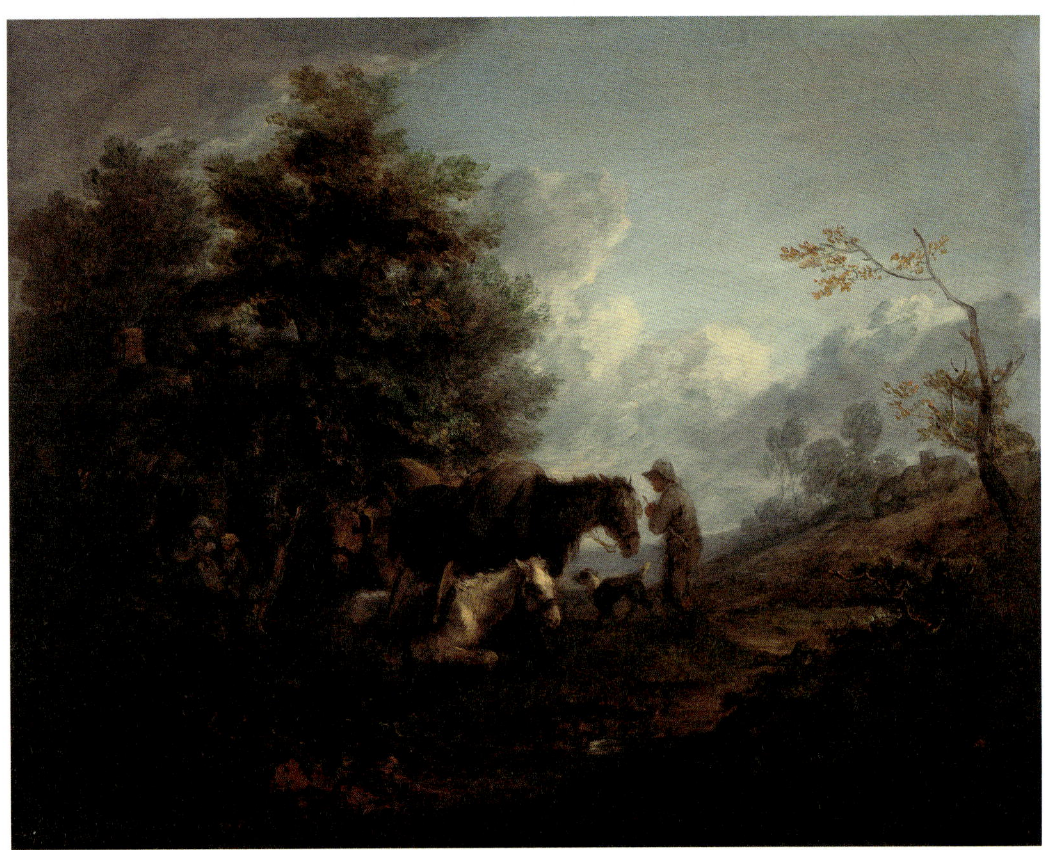

*Gainsborough's
Cottage Doors*

Art in Madison, Wisconsin (fig. 39). In the background, a vignette ancillary to the horses, dog and peasant placed in the centre of the canvas, is a group of figures, a mother with her children, huddled round a cottage door.

Much has been written about the theme of the 'cottage door' in Gainsborough's work. It was a theme that first appeared in about 1770 and it remained a subject to which he frequently returned. He first painted the *leitmotiv* in the large landscape originally owned by John, 2nd Viscount Bateman and now part of the Iveagh Bequest at Kenwood (fig. 40). As in the Madison landscape the cottage door theme takes an ancillary role in the composition and appears as a background detail. It is combined with another theme that recurs in the artist's work during his middle years, a group of packhorses and peasants travelling to or from market. Both subjects were further

Detail of fig. 39

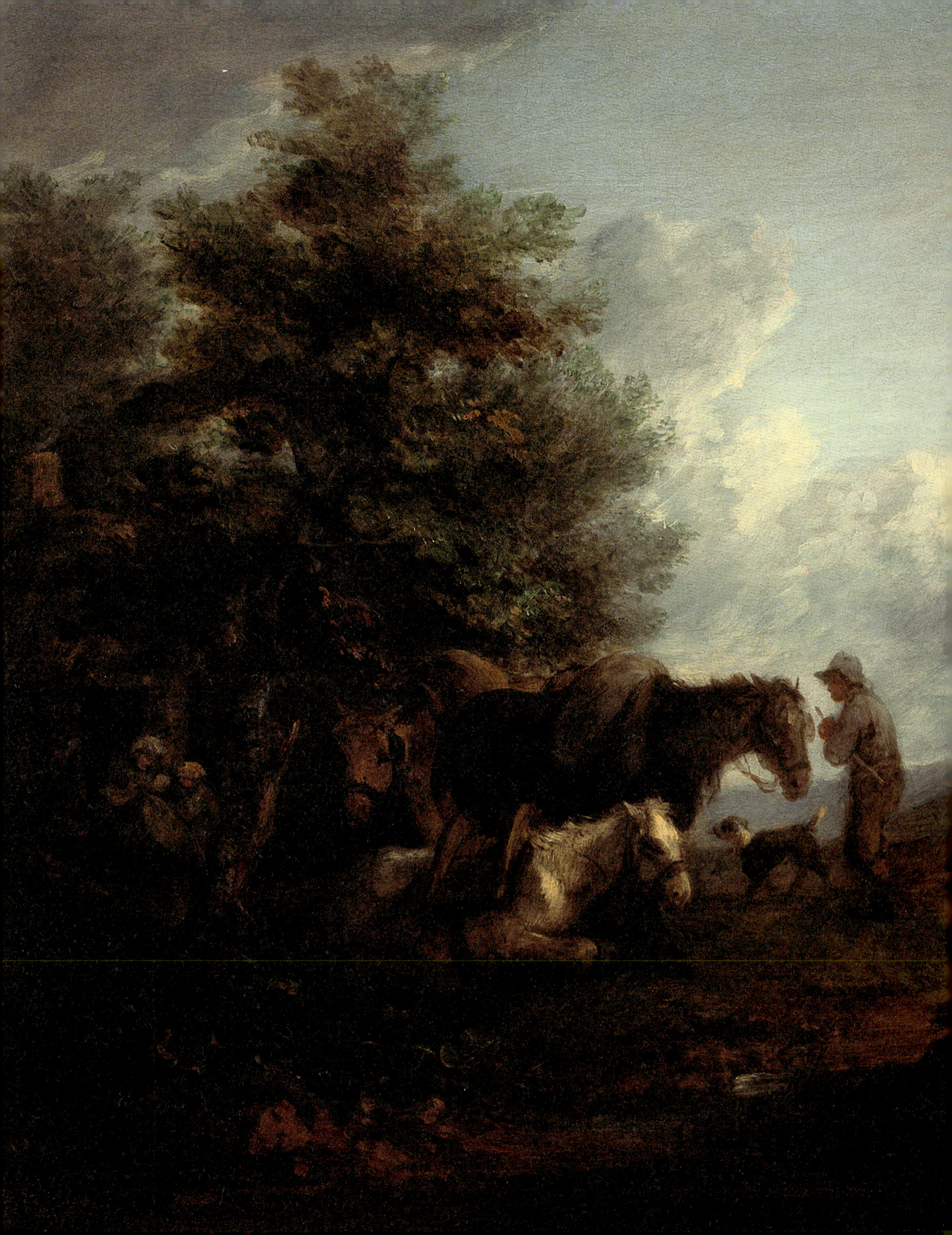

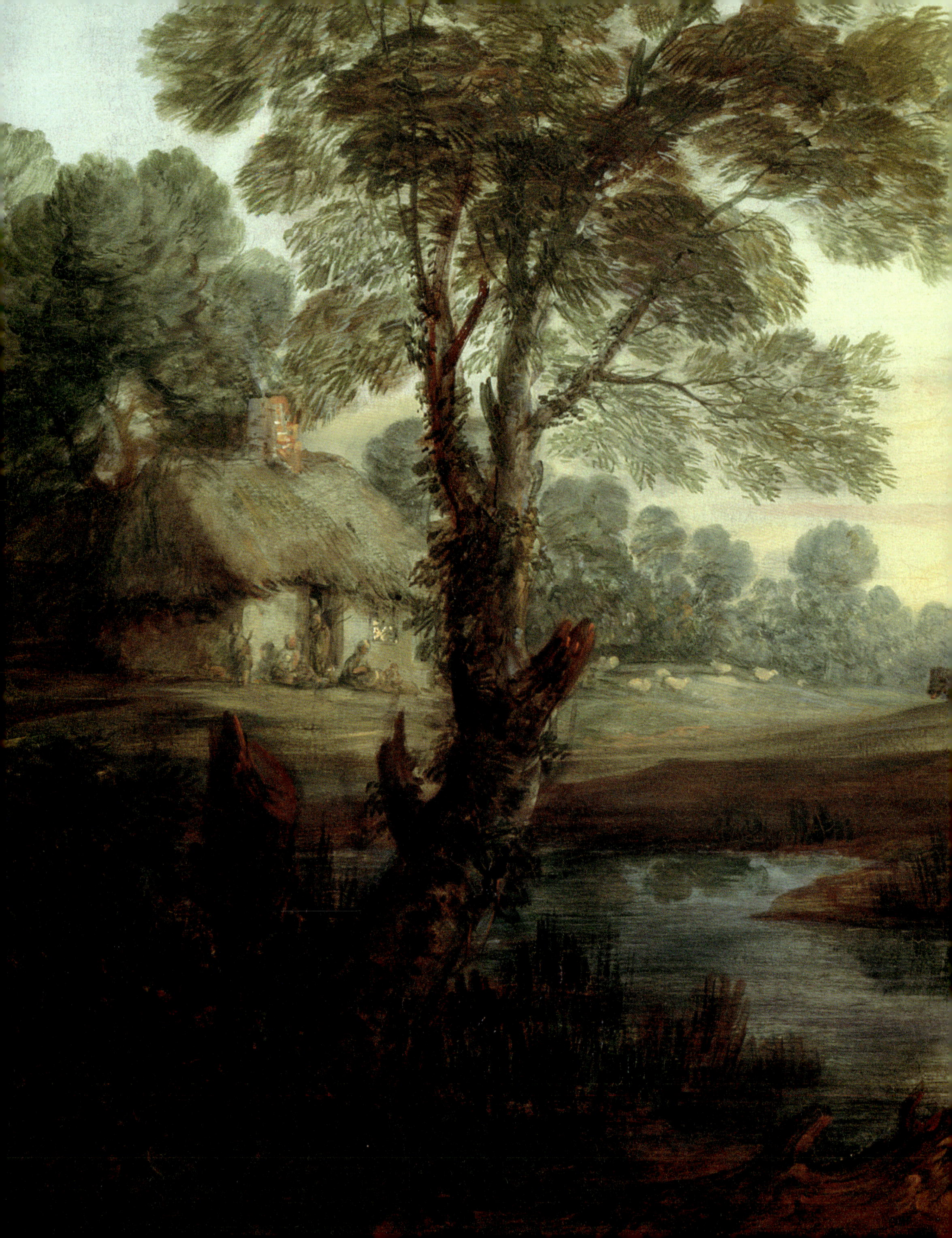

FIG. 40
Thomas Gainsborough
*Landscape with travellers returning
from market, c.* 1770
Oil on canvas, 119.4 × 146.1 cm
The Iveagh Bequest (English Heritage),
Kenwood House, London

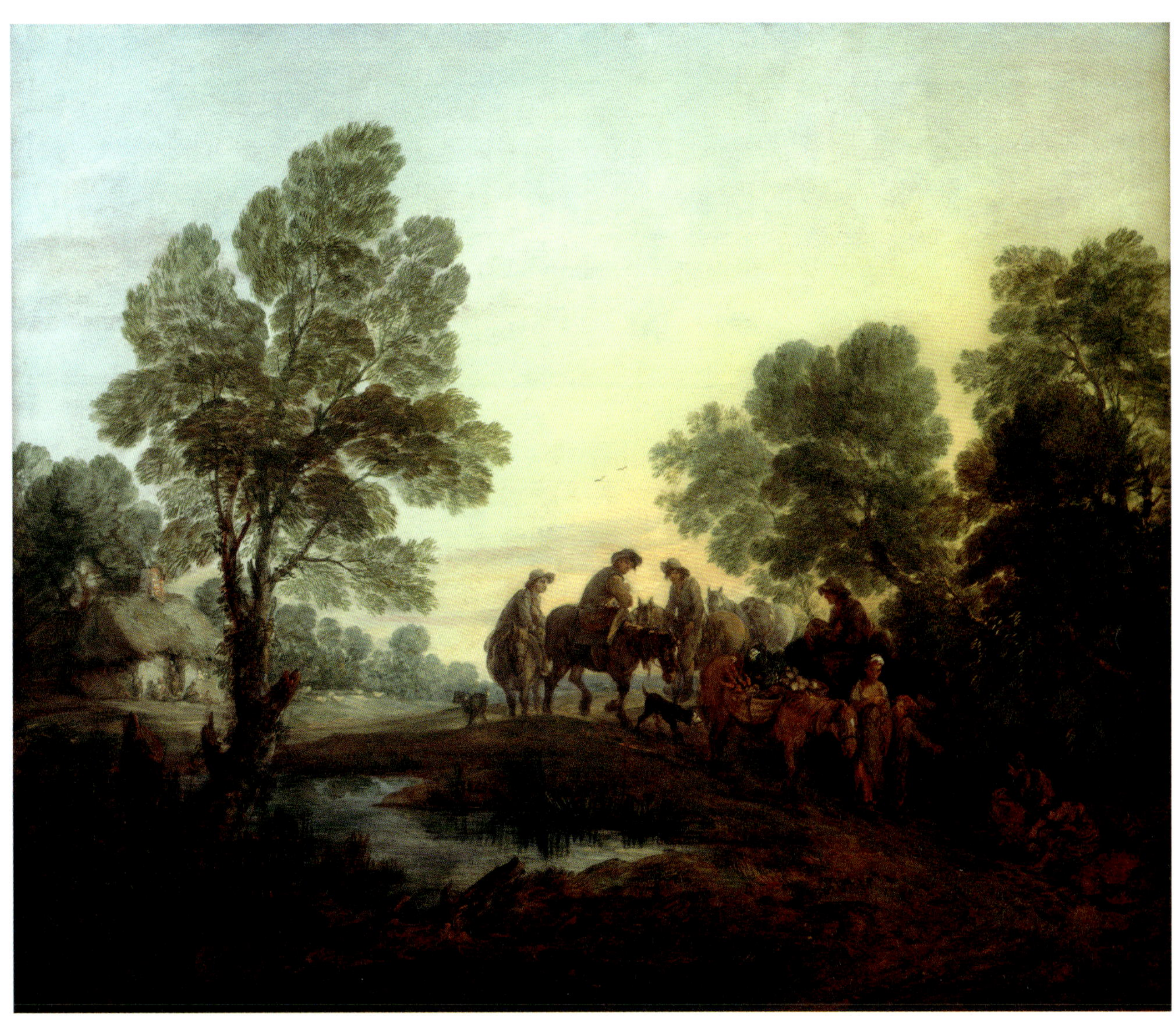

Detail of fig. 40

*Gainsborough's
Cottage Doors*

scrutinized and developed in a group of drawings made during the 1770s.

There are presently eighteen published drawings with a cottage door theme and Gainsborough no doubt produced many more that have disappeared during the intervening two hundred and fifty years. All the sheets vary in technique and content but each shows generations of women standing in a doorway accompanied by a group of boisterous children – from babes-in-arms to teenagers – enjoying each other's company and occasionally that of a playful dog. One drawing has a pigpen beside the house (fig. 41) and several have a couple of cows grazing a few yards away from the cottage. Others have an array of copper pans and earthenware pots spread out on the front steps of the cottage drying in the sunshine. The atmosphere is upbeat, fun-loving and carefree, and some sheets emphasize this jollity by including an additional figure that provides an opposing view of the world, one of toil and labour.

The drawing (fig. 41) can be dated to about 1776 and shows a development from an upright version of the subject known in two different versions, both of which date from about 1773. The first version was purchased from the artist by Charles, 4th Duke of Rutland and it has remained with his descendants at Belvoir Castle, and a replica, painted for Gainsborough's friend the violinist Felice de' Giardini, is now in the Tokyo Fuji Art Museum, Japan (fig. 42). The family gathered on the steps of the cottage on the left of the composition are strongly lit by the last rays of the evening sun and the laden woodman with his dog is placed in the centre of the canvas. An ancient tree beside the steps to the cottage is now overgrown and pollarded, to suggest the many generations that the cottage has been occupied by woodmen. One of the branches, jagged like a bolt of lightening,

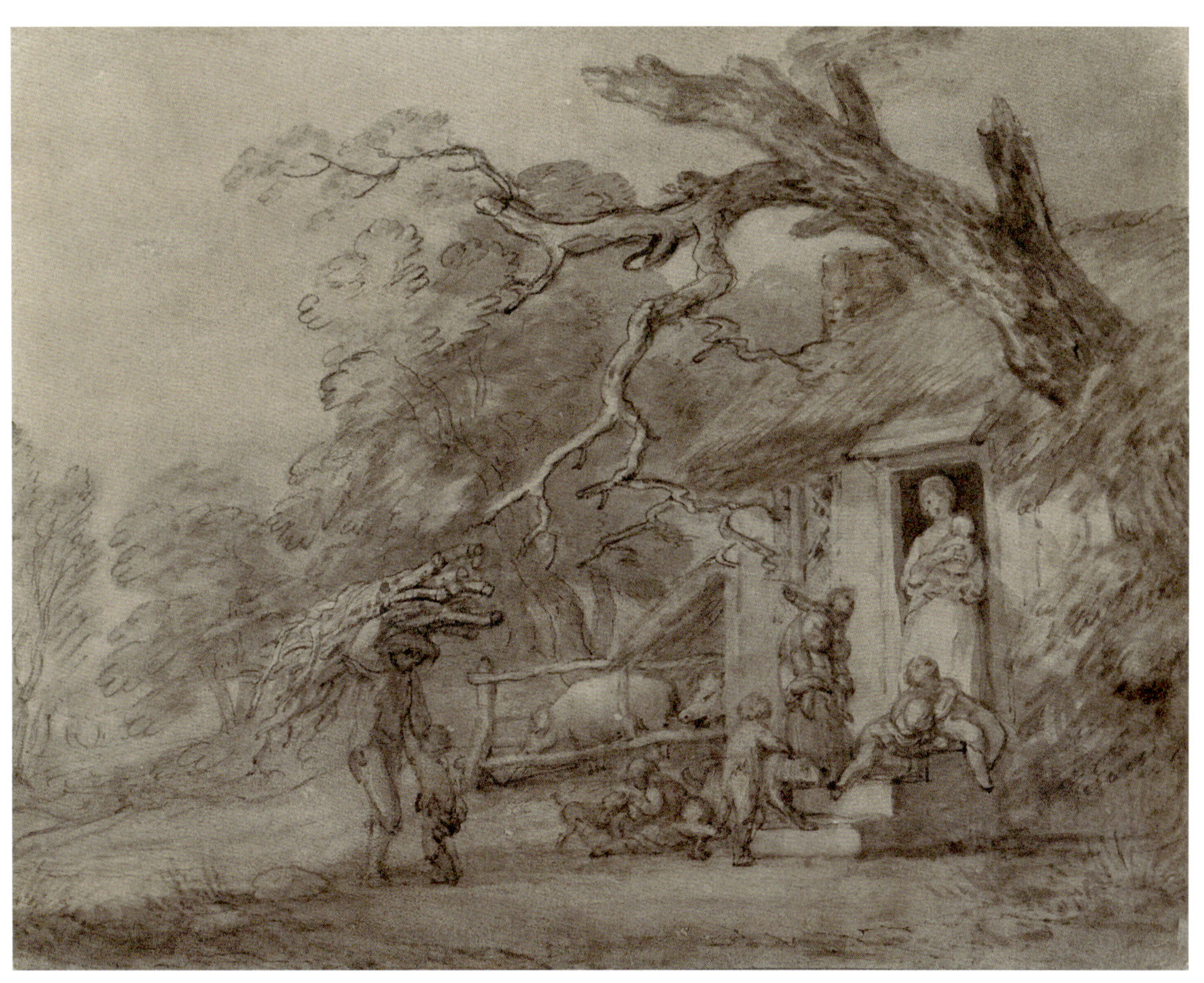

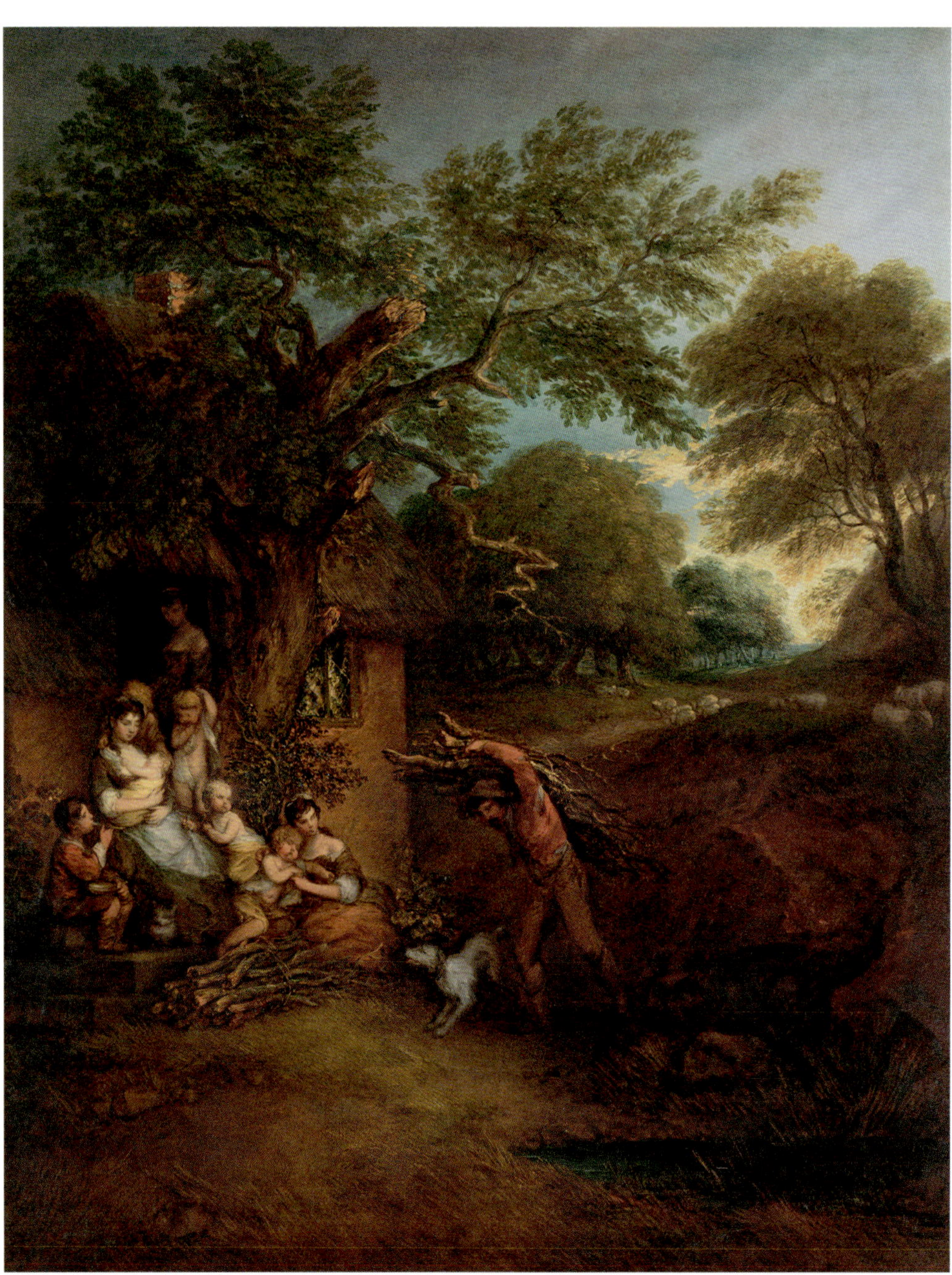

*Gainsborough's
Cottage Doors*

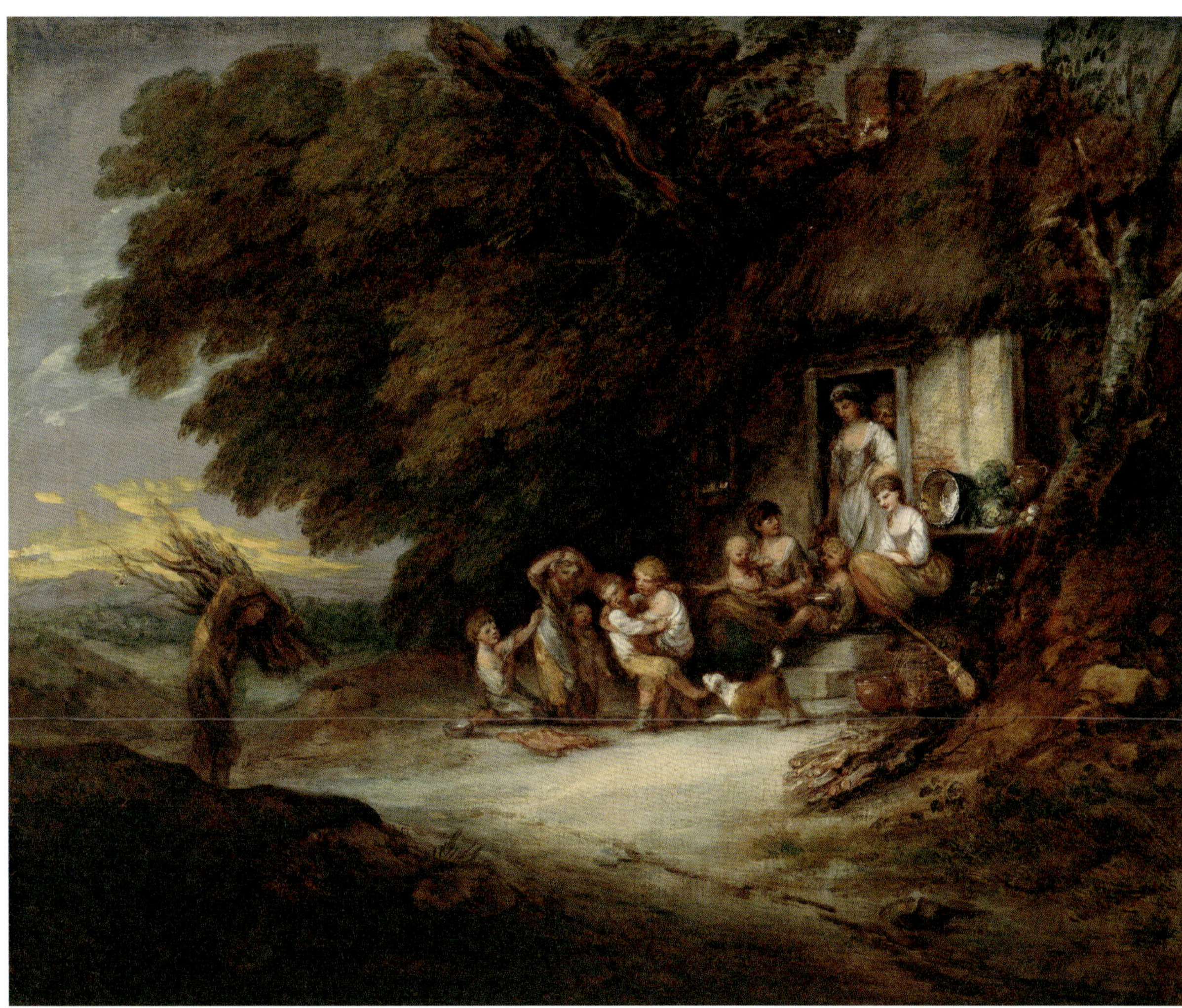

recalls a detail Gainsborough had first used in the painting etched
as *The Gipsies* in the 1750s.

Later on in the decade a second painting, now in Cincinnati
Art Museum (fig. 43), changed the format from upright to
horizontal and gave greater emphasis to the woodman. The

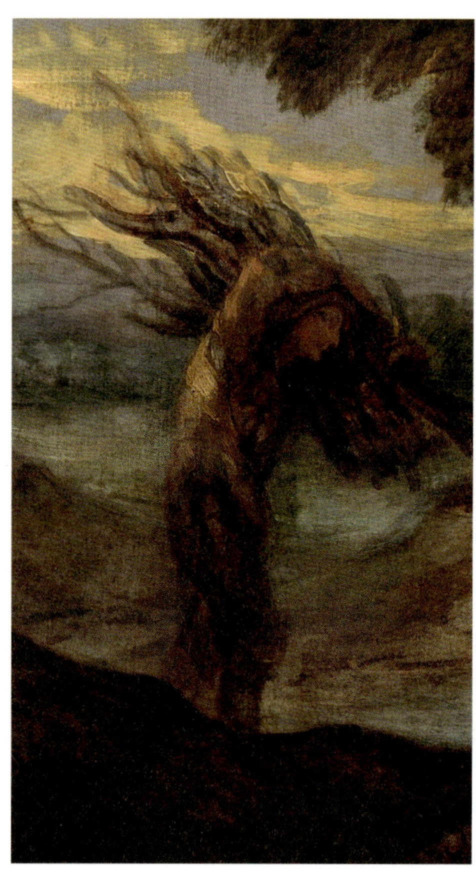

*Gainsborough's
Cottage Doors*

canvas was very probably one of the two landscapes shown at the Royal Academy in 1778, although, sadly, the notes published in contemporary newspapers are too general to confirm that this was so. One critic writing in the *General Evening Post* noted that the painting was "remarkable for the breadth and just distribution of the lights, the fine degradation of the distances, and the brilliancy and harmony of the colouring".[6] Another, a contributor to the *General Advertiser*, thought that "the *keeping* and *costume* of this piece are admirable. The *Distances* are judiciously managed, and the *light* is beautifully disposed. Such an union of strength and lightness is rarely found. The foreground is highly enriched, and the whole piece is full of nature."[7] In this canvas all the salient elements of the earlier landscape are emphasized. The woodman acts as a *repoussoir* figure bringing the beholder into the composition, there are more members of the family on the steps, they are more boisterous and demanding, and the tree is more ancient and dominates the cottage to a greater extent.

The addition of a male figure arriving at the homestead weighed down with an over-large bundle of sticks on his back reminds the viewer that the cottage chimney is smoking, an indication, like the pots and pans on the steps, of the domestic activity that has been going on, and of the material needs of the whole family. The contrast between toil and jollity, travel and rest, industry and idleness is clear. What is less certain is whether Gainsborough regarded the complete image as a metaphor for his own position and whether the relative marginalization of the male in these paintings was a mirror of his own outlook on life. He had a wife who, as the daughter (albeit illegitimate) of a duke, always had an overblown opinion of her own importance, and their two daughters appear to have inherited the same attitude and adopted a taste for expensive clothes. At the time both daughters were getting too old

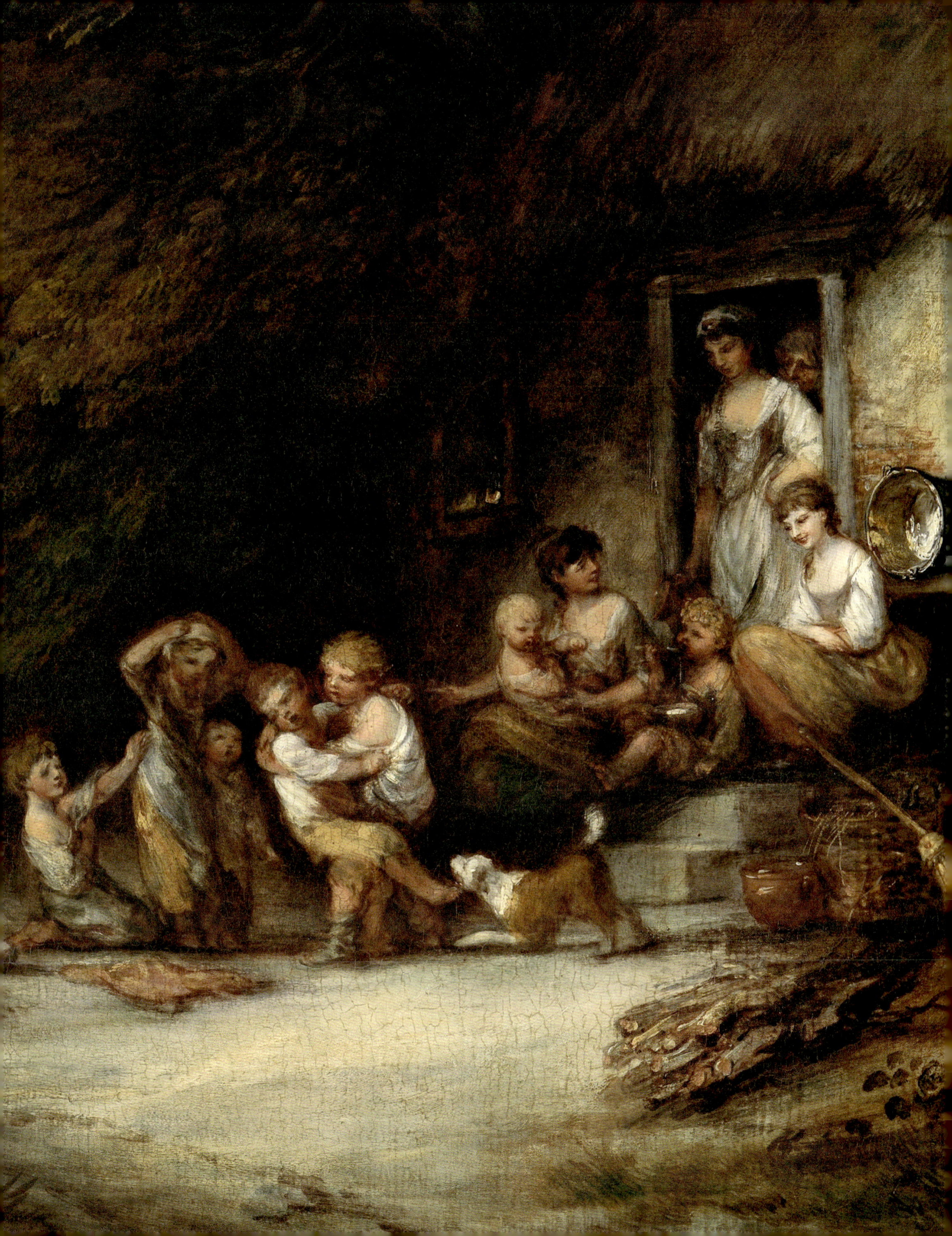

FIG. 44
Thomas Gainsborough
Diana and Actaeon, c. 1785
Oil on canvas, 158.1 × 188 cm
Royal Collection

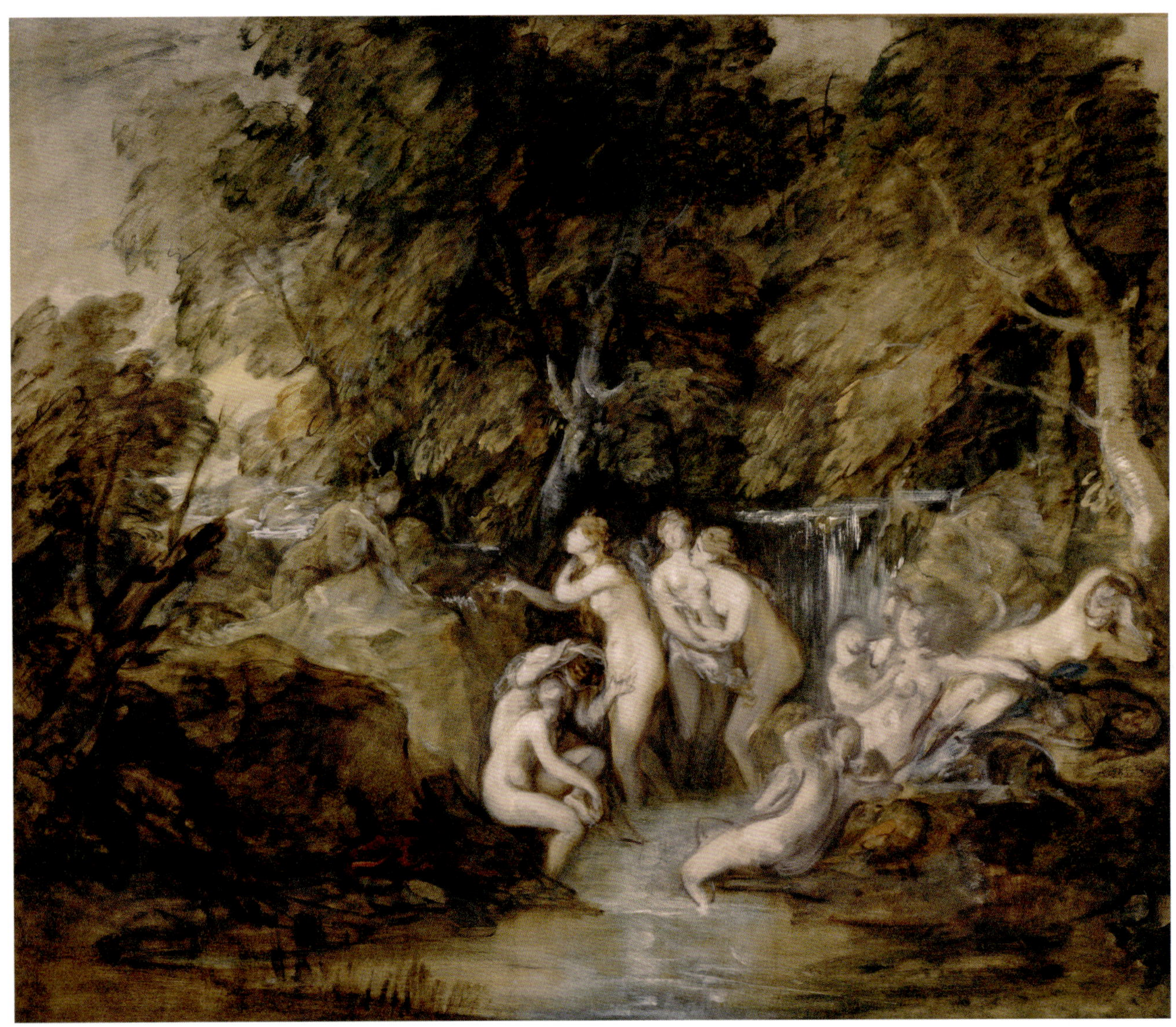

to look forward to the prospect of marriage with any confidence
and so they would continue to rely on their father's income.

There can be no doubt that Gainsborough was overly
protective of his two daughters, Mary and Margaret, or Mol and
the Captain as he nick-named them. His parental exasperation
over the circumstances of Mary's short-lived marriage are telling.
Her marriage to the oboist Johann Christian Fischer ended when
she was discovered buying "60 yards of White Satin for a Bed"
at Mr Mendham's shop at 24 Bond Street. From a neighbouring
shop she had also purchased lining, with the intention of
persuading a family friend, George Coyte, to sell all the fabric
at a profit for her to pocket, an act of profiteering that was then
regarded as a serious crime. We learn that her mother intended
to "smother it", while the artist felt otherwise, but made do with
sharing his disquiet with his sister, Mary Gibbon.[8] Back in
Sudbury in the middle 1780s another of his sisters, Sarah, whose
second son, Gainsborough Dupont, had lived with his uncle since
boyhood, was charged with monitoring an allowance to their
impoverished brother John, who was known as 'Scheming' Jack
after his worthless inventions. So Gainsborough was responsible
not only for his immediate family but also for some of his siblings
and their offspring. It must have seemed a heavy burden akin to
the weighty bundle of sticks shown in some representations of the
cottage door.

The same metaphor may also have been behind his choice
of subject for the extraordinary late painting *Diana and
Actaeon* (fig. 44). The existence of the painting was unknown –
presumably the artist never showed it to Bate, who would have
found the opportunity to write about it – until it was discovered
in his studio after the artist's death. The subject of the painting
is taken from Ovid's *Metamorphoses*. When Actæon was hunting

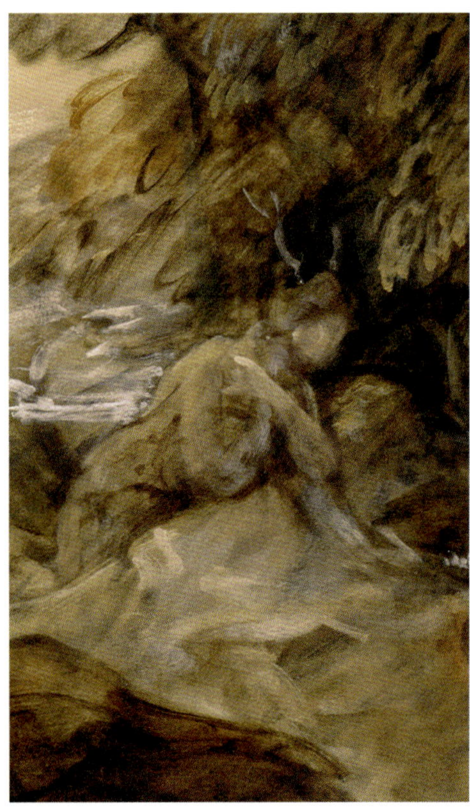

*Gainsborough's
Cottage Doors*

in the woods, he came across the goddess Diana bathing with her attendants. Diana threw water into the mortal's face, turning him into a stag, and he was torn apart by his own hounds. In Gainsborough's painting Diana and her nymphs are given centre stage surrounded by dense woodland, bathing in a plunge pool created by a waterfall. Diana's arm, deliberately ill-defined and out of focus, shows her movement as she splashes water towards a faceless figure leaning towards the pool. Actaeon's arms are crossed over his breast, accepting his destiny like an annunciate Virgin, and his nascent antlers, the first indications of his fate, are almost lost in the arboreous splendour enveloping the scene. Despite the violence of the story, Gainsborough's painting has an extraordinary quality of inevitability, calmness and grace.

The subject has many parallels with the cottage door theme, especially that of a man in isolation. By adapting the metaphor to the Ovidian story, Gainsborough might well parallel a development in his own perception of his personal situation. If the equation is between Diana and her nymphs and Gainsborough's wife and his family, then spouse and daughters are driving the artist to an early grave.[9] But, as one might expect, the painting includes other significant aesthetic considerations.

Diana and Actaeon is often described, incorrectly, as unfinished. As a work designed to gratify no one but the painter, this conclusion seems simplistic. It was presumably completed enough to satisfy Gainsborough and in this particular case the lyricism and the unfocused quality of the painting provide a studied imprecision in the storytelling. It is perhaps instructive to compare it to the copies of Old Master paintings that the artist made earlier in his career. One painting by Van Dyck, like the theme of the cottage door, was revisited several times.

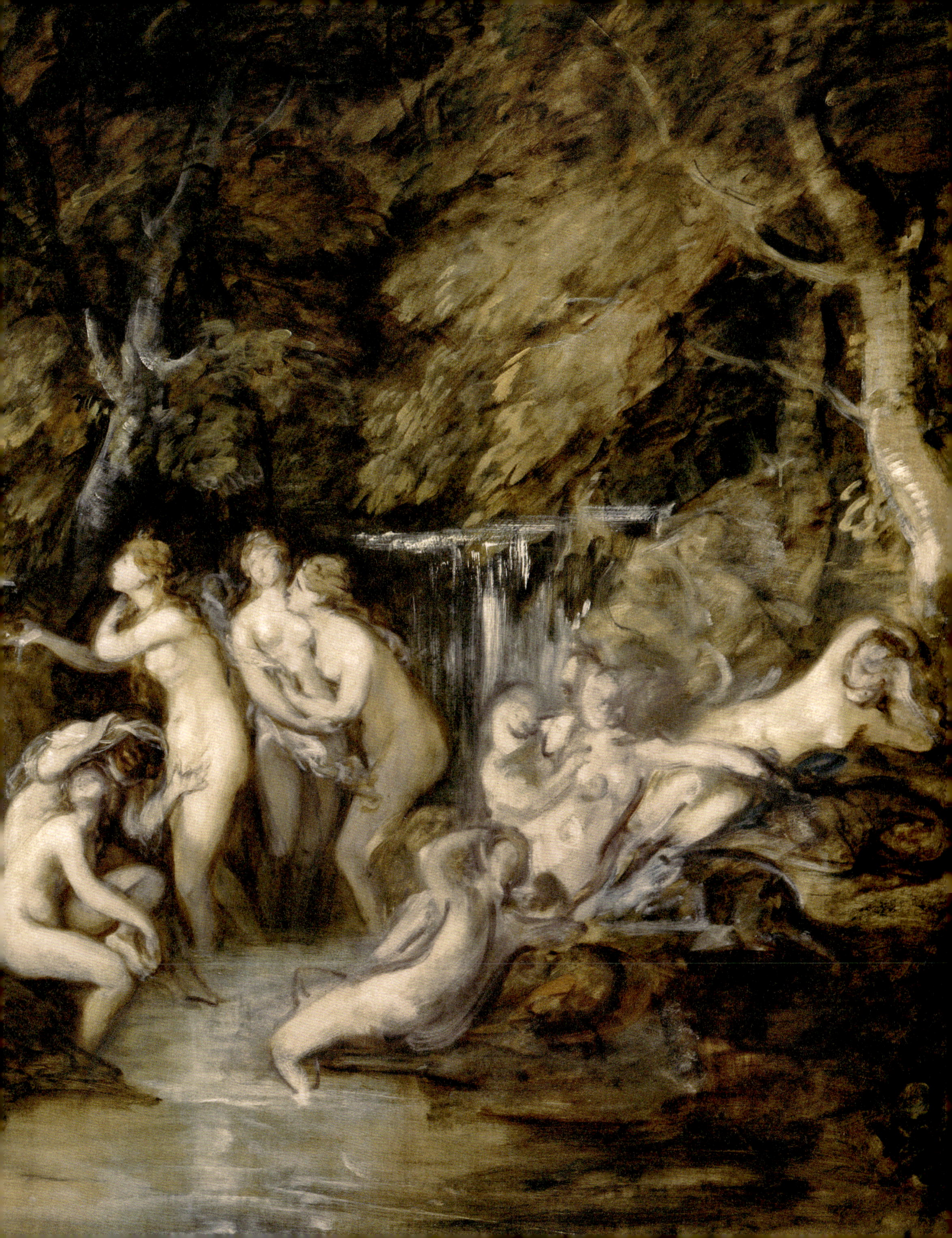

In 1765 Gainsborough painted Theodosia Magill, the charge of John, 3rd Earl of Darnley, who, through her marriage, was to become the Countess of Clanwilliam. At the time Gainsborough was working for Darnley he must have seen Van Dyck's canvas of Lord John and Lord Bernard Stuart in the peer's London house, and it had a lasting effect on the artist. More than any other such image it is charged with the romance of the seventeenth-century royalist cause and suffused by the spectator with the knowledge that both brothers were killed in the British Civil War shortly after sitting for their portraits. The original portrait by Van Dyck is now in the National Gallery in London and a full-size copy by Gainsborough is in the St Louis Art Museum. Unsatisfied, however, with the lesson he had learned from a single copy, Gainsborough returned to the portrait and made further reproductions of it. Some were of the head of Lord Bernard and others focused on his costume, though instead of using the rich blue of the sitter's cloak and his breeches he continued to use the silver of the rest of the costume (fig. 45). Like the canvas of *Diana and Actæon*, the copy, now in a private collection, is not, in conventional terms, finished. Instead, it is as complete as Gainsborough wished it to be. As Gainsborough was so enamoured with the work of his seventeenth-century mentor, in choosing to paint copies after Van Dyck he was not only performing an act of homage, but also attempting to learn a series of lessons. Quite naturally each copy emphasizes a different aspect of the example Van Dyck had to offer.

The partial review of Gainsborough's career in this study has concentrated on a limited number of aspects of his creativity and on his highly principled opinions about what contemporary art should attempt and, perhaps more clearly, what it should not. It has examined his strategies for ridding himself of the constraints

FIG. 45
Thomas Gainsborough
Lord Bernard Stuart after
Anthony van Dyck, c. 1765
Oil on canvas, 113 × 86.5 cm
Private collection

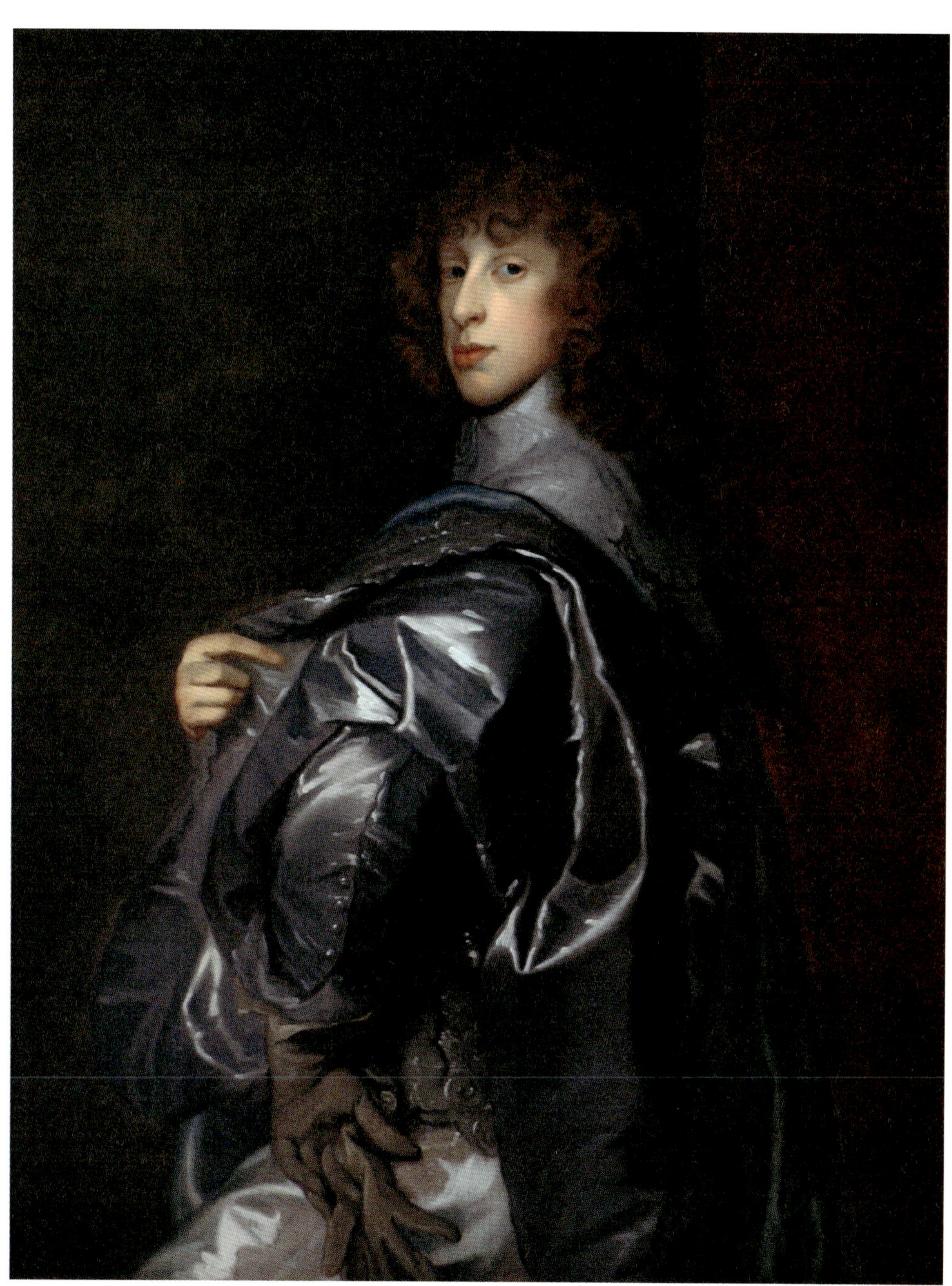

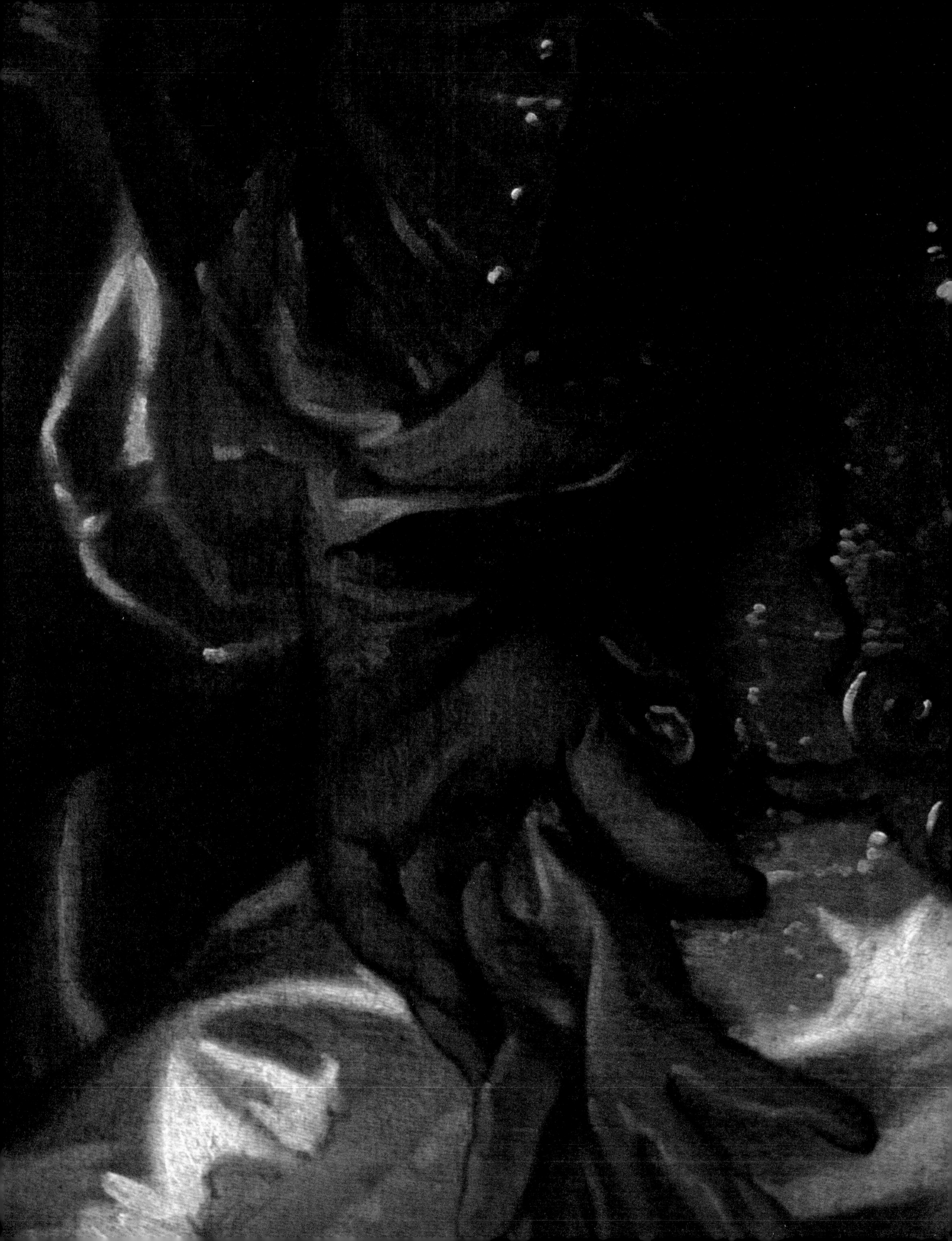

imposed by the Academy; the varying degree of finish in his works; his use of repetition and his concern, perhaps even lack of confidence, in constructing compositions. This all provides a very useful background to our understanding of no less than two additional versions that have recently come to light of the famous canvas of *The Cottage Door* that he showed at the Royal Academy in 1780, a painting which is now in The Huntington, San Marino, (cat. 1).

When the landscape was shown at the Royal Academy it attracted surprisingly little comment from the press. The 1780 exhibition was the first presented in the Academy's new premises in Somerset House and the event was regarded as important enough that a book should be produced criticizing the exhibits. The author of *A Candid Review of the Exhibition* showed a preference for the 'fancy' pictures and felt that in the case of the *Cottage Door* Gainsborough had "neglected his Landscape to display the whole force of his genius in a beautiful group of children and their mother".[10] Another critic writing in a contemporary newspaper was more flattering: "This beautiful scene where serenity and pleasure dwell in every spot, and the lovely figures composed in the finest rural style, their situation worthy of them, forms a scene of happiness that may truly be called Adam's paradise".[11] Later commentators identified the female figure as a likeness of Georgiana, Duchess of Devonshire, which perhaps says more about the status of the painting and the celebrity of the duchess than it reveals of Gainsborough's own intentions. However, the assurance of the figure, her confidence and her satisfaction with her lot invest her with an undeniable nobility, which is strengthened by the powerful triangular composition. The painting was originally conceived as a standard 40 by 50 inch canvas painted with the long side of

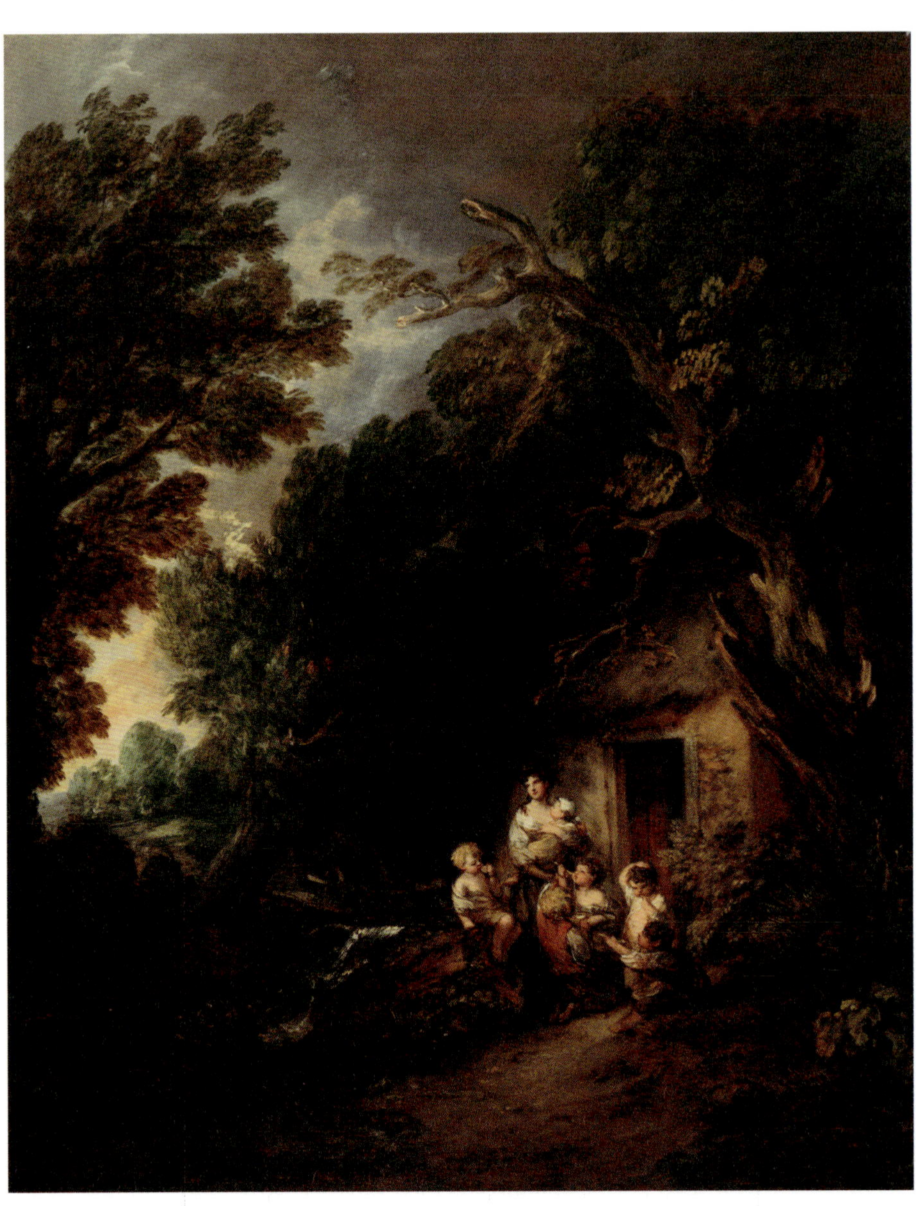

*Gainsborough's
Cottage Doors*

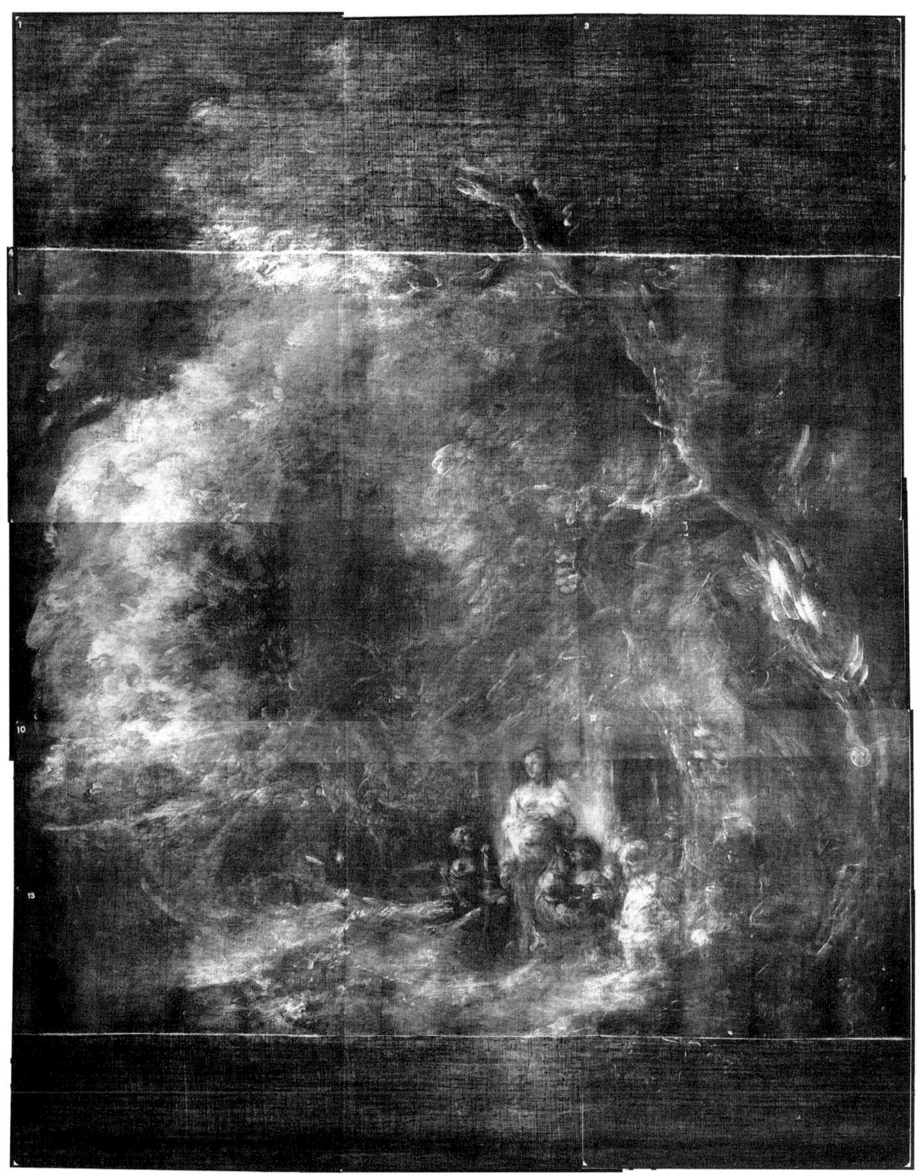

the composition at the bottom, which links it to the Cincinnati landscape painted two years earlier. Clearly Gainsborough's enthusiasm spread beyond the confines of his original canvas, so he added a foot-wide strip of canvas to the top and another seven-inch strip at the bottom, as can be seen in the X-ray of the painting (fig. 47). These changes enabled the painter to continue the lines of the trees and to echo the triangular shape of the figure group, which, as an afterthought, he reinforced by adding the boy leaning forward, arms outstretched on the extreme right. On the right is a gnarled, hollow tree that had become a constituent part of this subject, and on the left a pair of pollarded willow trees grow on either side of a fast-flowing stream. The group of figures and its relationship to the landscape must have preyed on the artist's mind and he revisited the composition twice more before his death.[12]

Both repetitions of the *Cottage Door* are less finished than the landscape in The Huntington. The painting in the collection of James Stunt (cat. 2) is on a reused canvas which, X-rays have shown (fig. 49), had first been used for an entirely different image that included a classical façade, seen faintly at the top right, that is reminiscent of the buildings in the painting now known as *Charity relieving Distress* (private collection, on loan to Gainsborough's House, Sudbury), which was first painted in 1784 and altered by the artist three years later. Reusing a canvas implies that Gainsborough was limiting his expenses, which supports the idea that the landscape was painted for Gainsborough's own amusement rather than as a work he intended to sell.

Compared to the Huntington landscape, the Stunt version is painted in a more cursory way: like the copies after Van Dyck, it was intended to satisfy Gainsborough rather than a patron. The colour is more muted, with fewer tones used to define the forms,

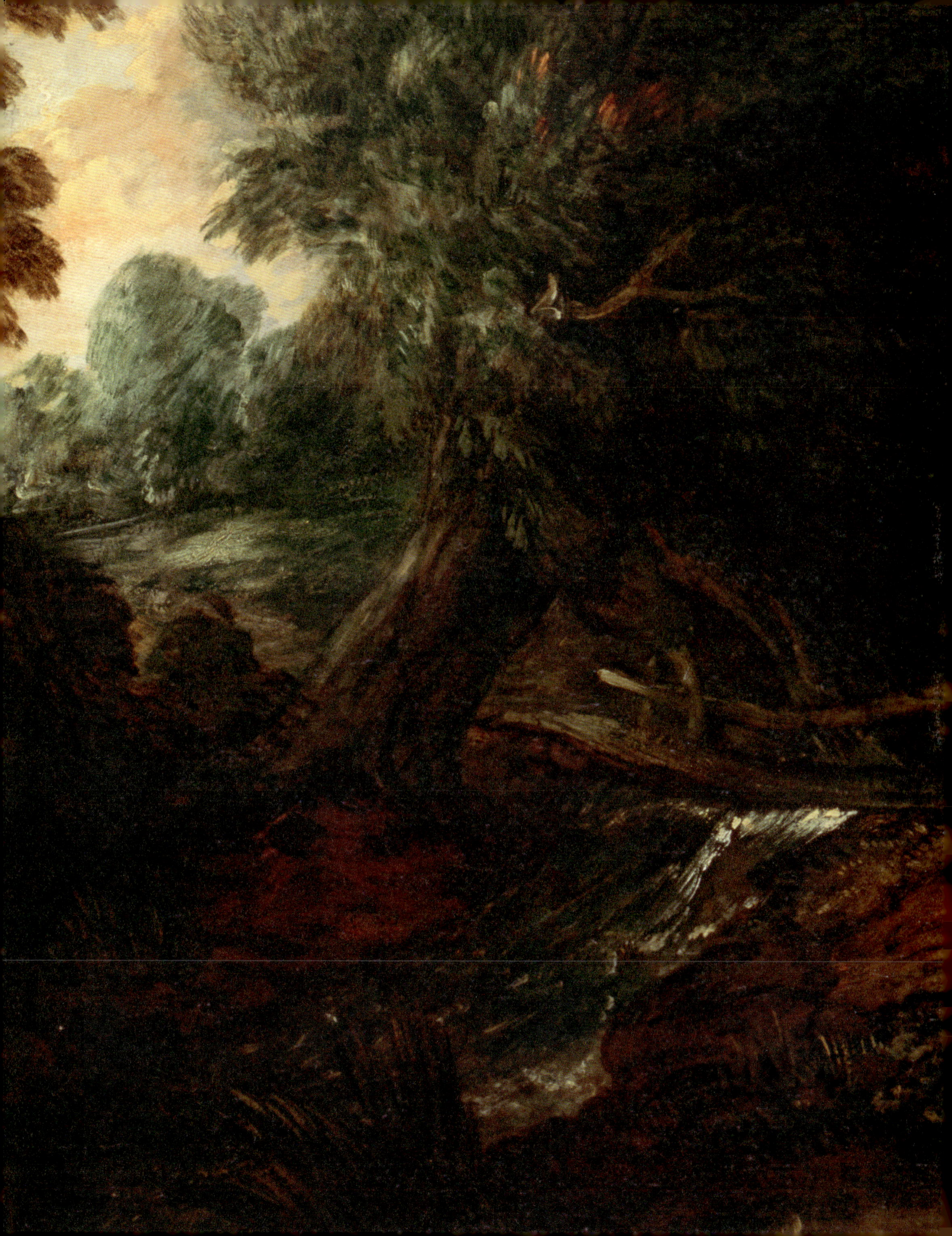

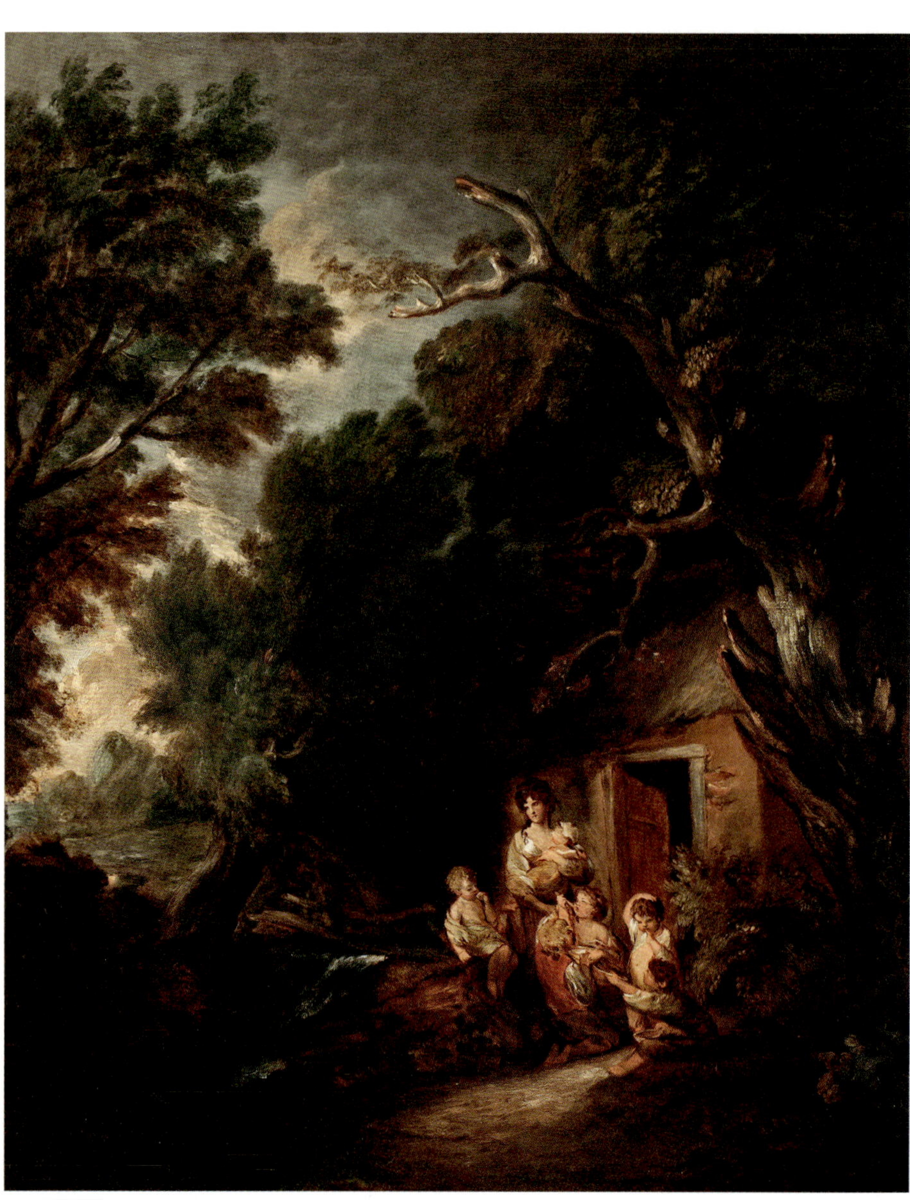

FIG. 49
X-ray of the Stunt *Cottage Door* (cat. 2) and
detail showing the location of the buildings
of a previous composition beneath the
present surface

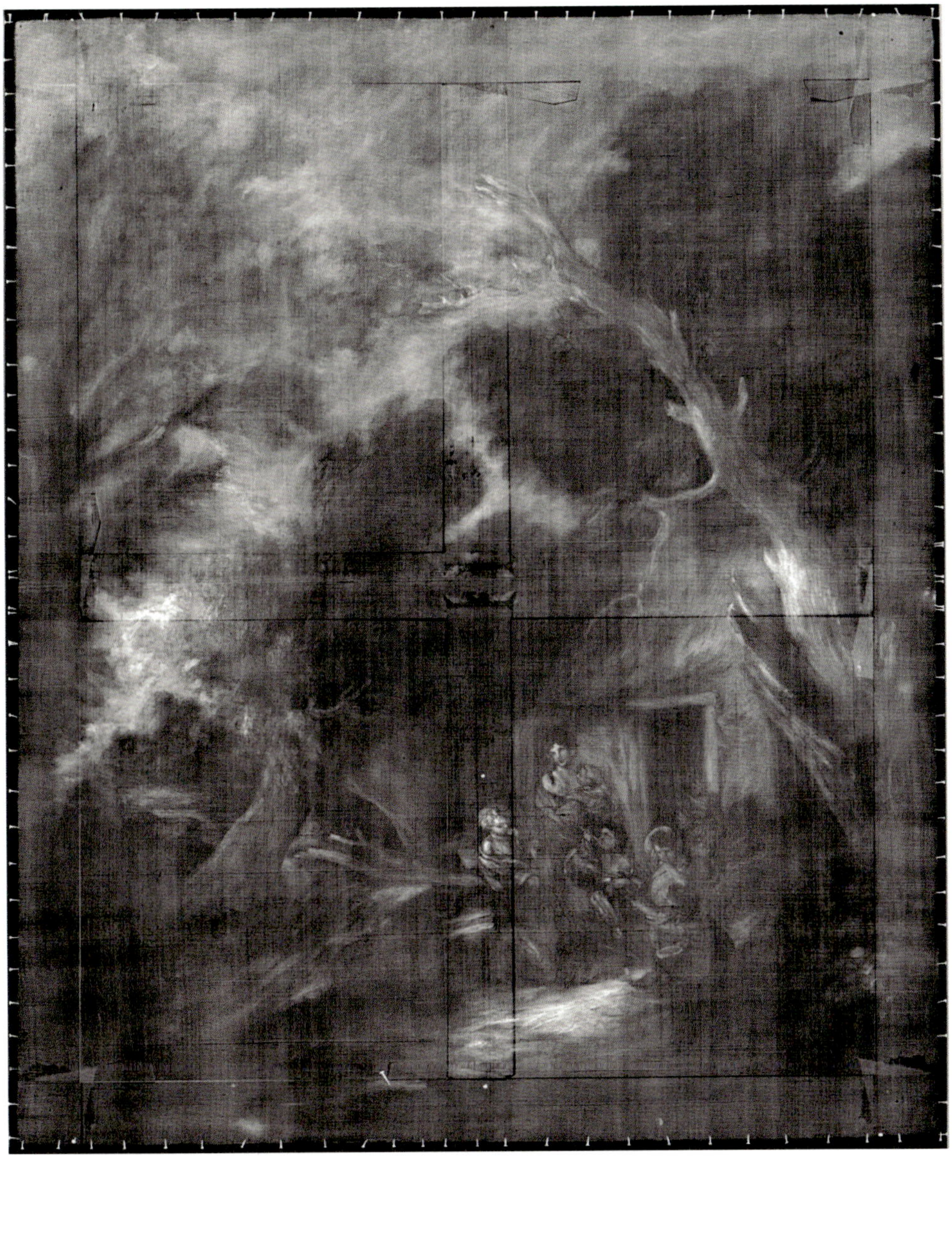

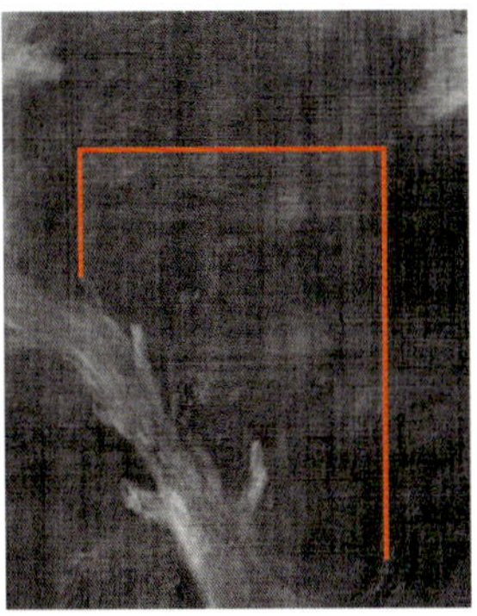

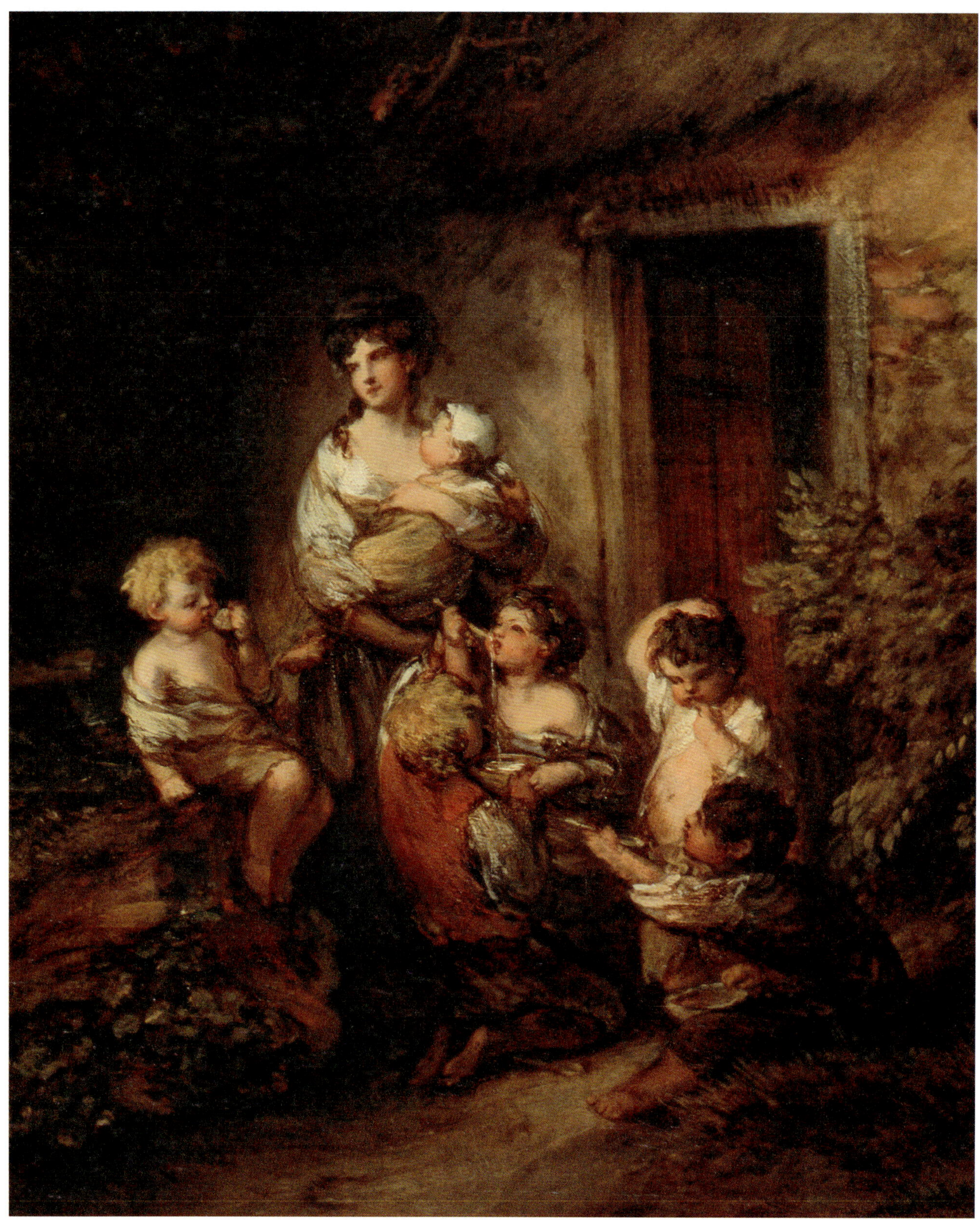

Detail of the Huntington *Cottage Door* (cat. 1)

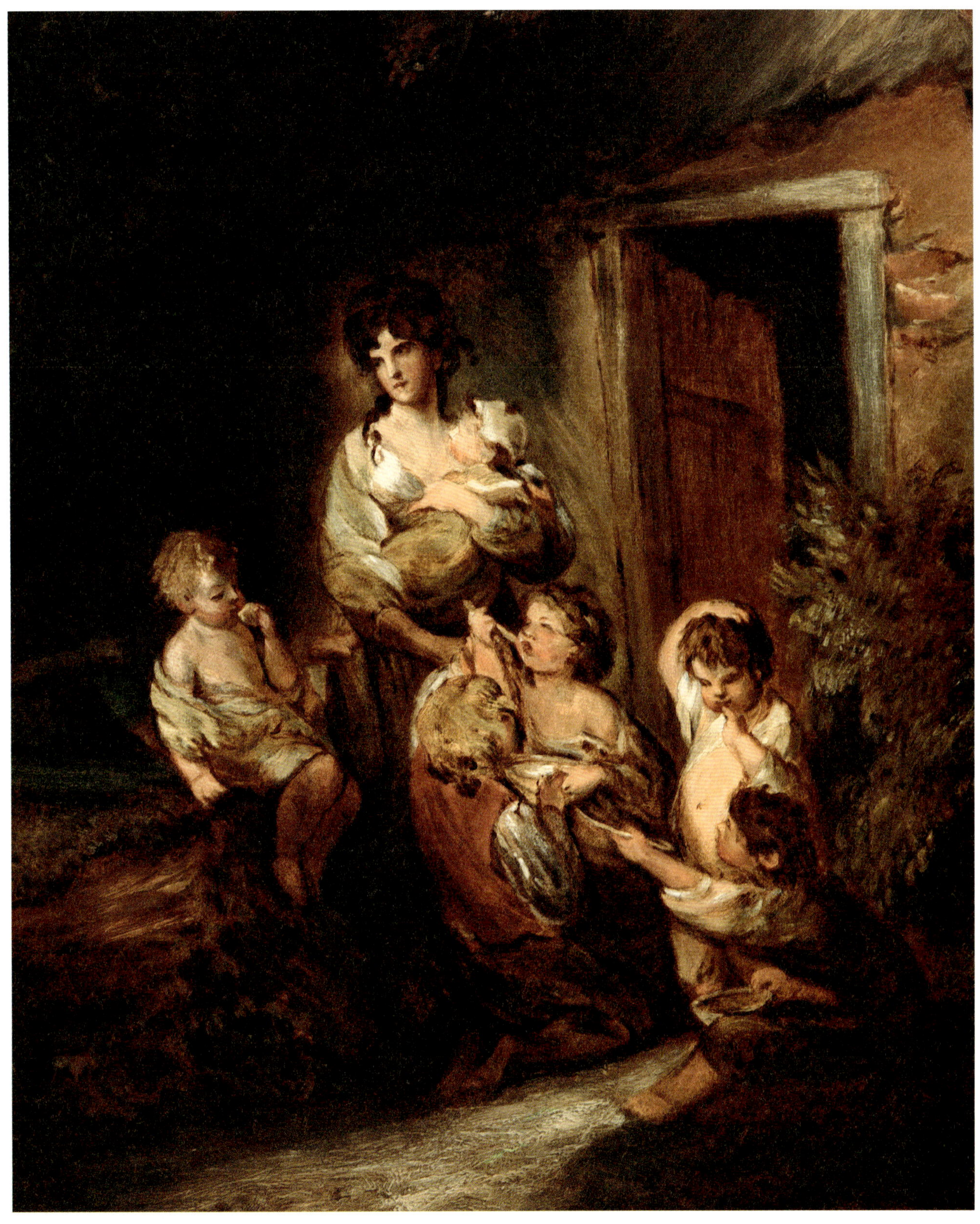

Detail of the Stunt *Cottage Door* (cat. 2)

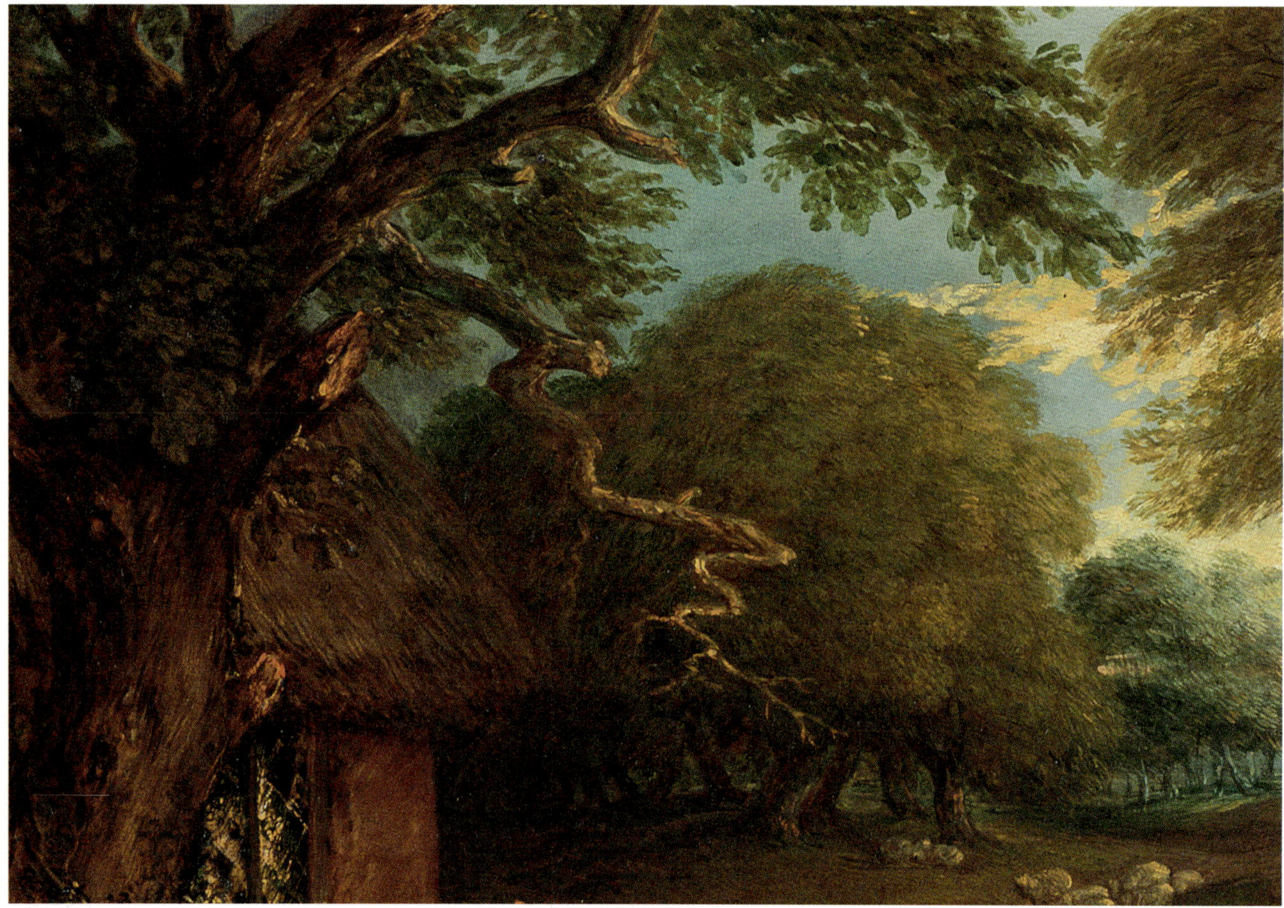

Detail of the Fuji *Wooded landscape* (fig. 42)

Gainsborough's
Cottage Doors

but the draughtsmanship is as confident as ever with every mark
defining the forms, a trait that is especially true in the painting
of the figure group. Like the critic writing in *A Candid Review*,
Gainsborough must have been content with the figure group and
instead turned his attention to the landscape and the lighting. In
this version he gives a different emphasis to the landscape, toying
with the gap between the trees immediately above the heads of the
figures and creating a shape that appears to extend the branches of
the dead tree on the right and recalls the dead branch in the Tokyo
landscape (fig. 42). Using greener tones than he had used in the
1780 painting, he extended the foliage at the bottom of the tree on
the left and used less blue in the paint mix he used for the trees on
the horizon. The flecks of yellow defining the foliage on the all-
but-dead tree on the right are absent in the Stunt version, a feature
which focuses the eye on the figure group in the centre.

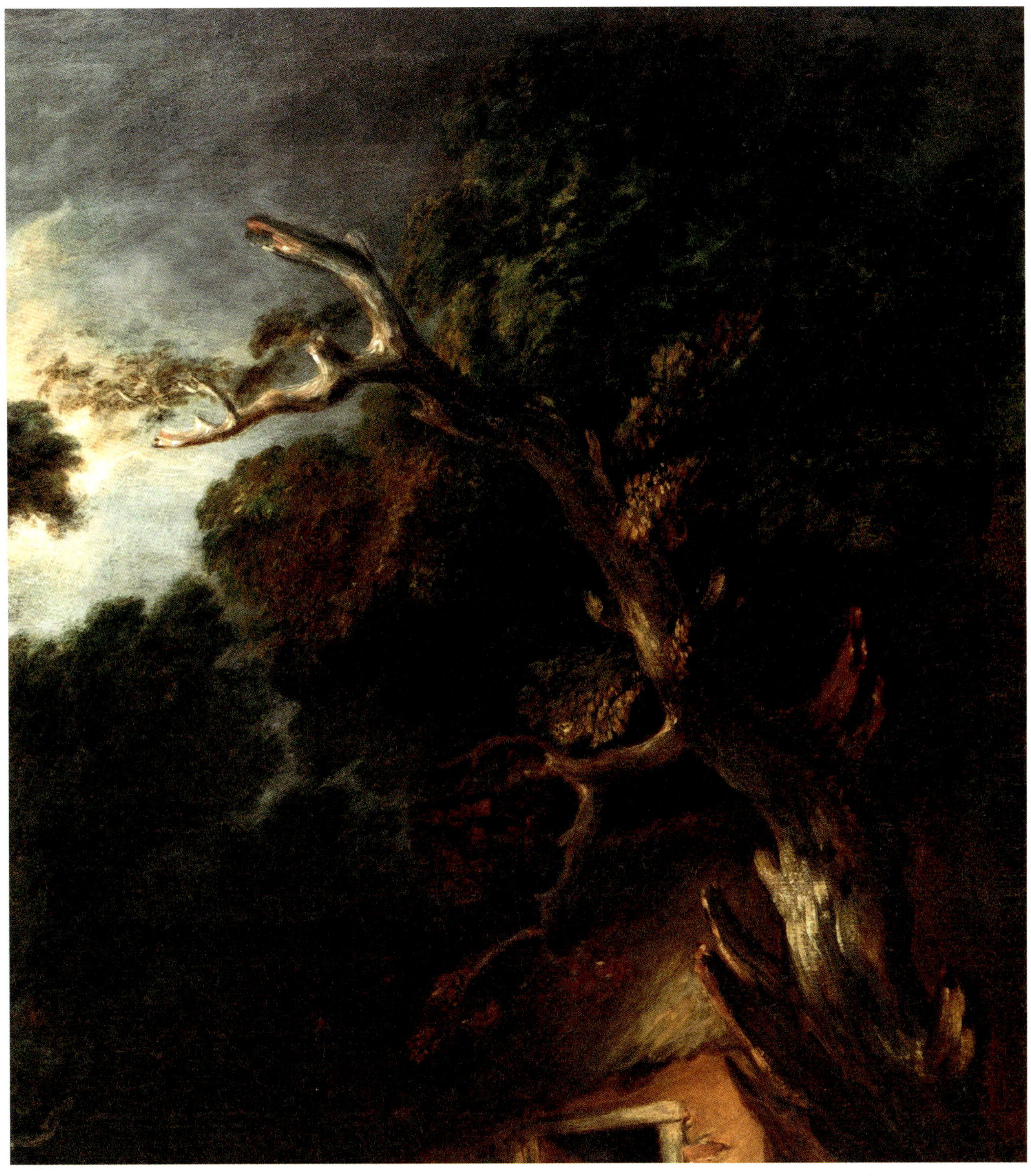

Detail of the Stunt *Cottage Door* (cat. 2)

The third version of the *Cottage Door* (cat. 3), in a private collection in Dallas, is painted in a lighter key using a palette closer to the one the painter used in his *Greyhounds chasing a fox* (The Iveagh Bequest, Kenwood), which was painted in about 1785. The tones of the field and trees in the background and the willow are very similar to the Kenwood painting, though the agitated whimsy of the trees has, in the five years since Gainsborough painted the original version of the *Cottage Door*, become more effete and wind-blown. The Dallas painting is also more sketchy in its handling and the figure group is little more than blocked in. The handling, especially given the darkening of the pigments that has inevitably occurred in the other two versions of the canvas, gives a greater clarity to the composition, though it lacks the crystal focus of The Huntington's painting. Much less formal than the other two versions, it is also less probing and has none of the experimentation of the Stunt version.

Shortly before he died Gainsborough revisited the *Cottage Door* once again (fig. 50). This monumental revised version of the subject is now on loan to the Getty Museum from the University of California in Los Angeles. In this canvas the cottage has become further subsumed into the background foliage, and the diagonal tree, deader and more menacing, frames the figure group. By contrast to any of the other renderings of this subject, this group now includes the peasant father. He sits on his bundle of logs and relaxes smoking a clay pipe. The mother, in an identical pose to the Huntington version, cradles her new-born child. She has lost all her claims to being a duchess and returned to the peasantry. Her toddler son and daughter are in poses similar to those in the Huntington canvas; the other children are replaced by the father figure, and the formality of the triangular composition has given way to a more egalitarian group. The curves of the tree

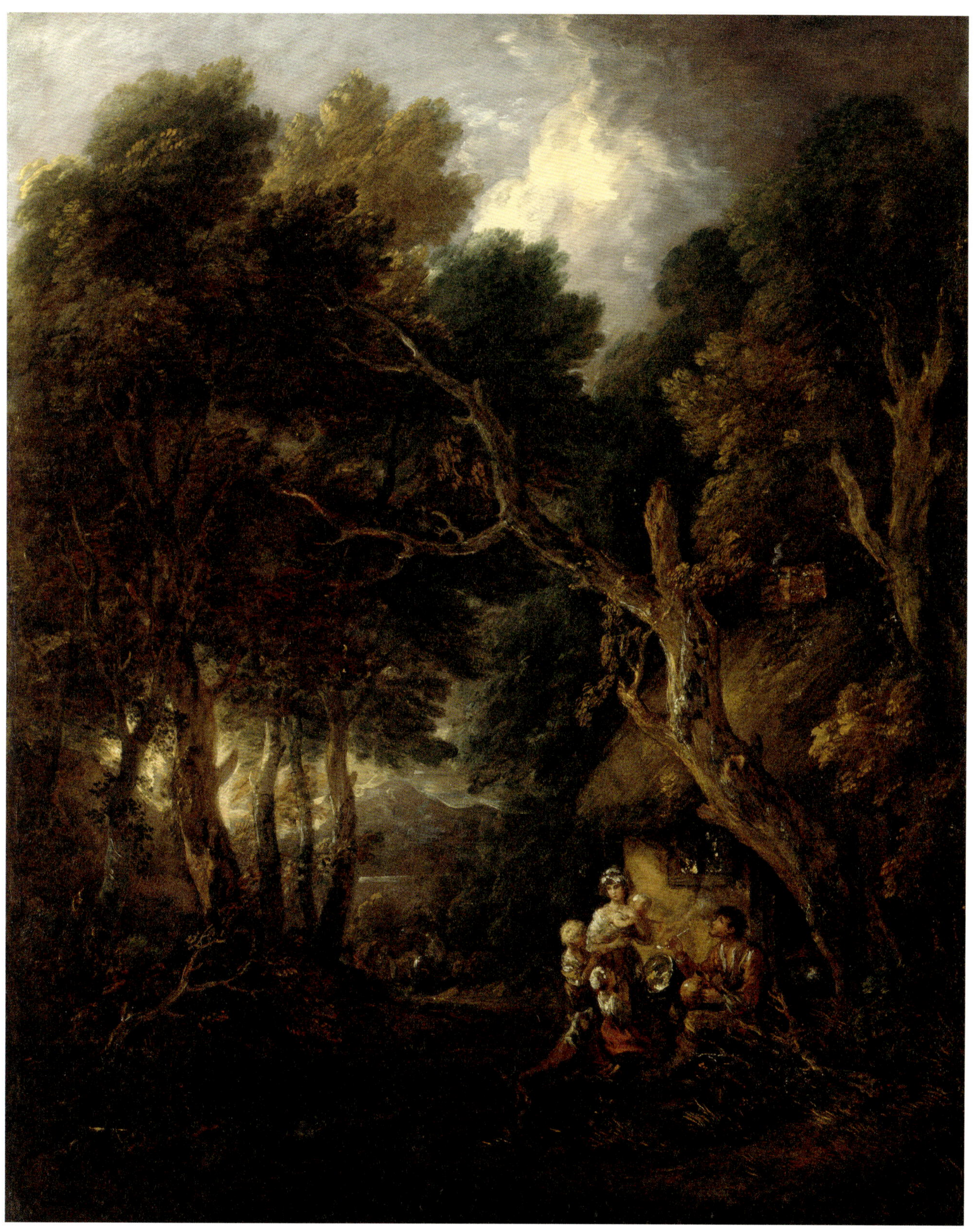

trunks on the left bring a frivolity to the scene and the distant view, cut off by the silhouette of a mountain, increases the intimacy of the composition. It is a perfect union between the natural and the human worlds and it is tempting to think that the telling alterations to the staffage and the subtle changes in the landscape are a reflection of the artist's personal tranquillity in the closing months of his life.

The significance of the *Cottage Door* theme, painted over nearly twenty years, not only provides an invaluable insight into the artist's personality and his very worrying concerns but also relates to the private and public aspects of his work. Showing these three versions of the landscape together will help the visitor to appreciate Gainsborough's extraordinary facility as a painter and the complexity and variety of his approach to painting.

Notes

1   John Hayes, *The Letters of Thomas Gainsborough*, New Haven and London 2001, p. 194.
2   Letter to William, 2nd Earl of Dartmouth, dated 13 April 1771: Hayes 2001, p. 90.
3   John Hayes, *Gainsborough*, London 1975, p. 46.
4   *Morning Herald*, 17 January 1785.
5   The changes to the portrait of Mrs Sheridan with accompanying X-ray and infrared images are detailed by Carol Christensen and Eleonora Luciano in 'The Evolution of Gainsborough's Portrait of Elizabeth Sheridan', *Burlington Magazine*, CLV, April 2013, pp. 238–42. Details of the changes the artist made to the portrait of 'Perdita' Robinson are awaiting publication.
6   30 April – 2 May 1778, p. 4. The description is of both this painting and the other exhibited landscape and upright canvas at Belvoir Castle: John Hayes, *The Landscape Paintings of Thomas Gainsborough*, 2 vols., London 1982, pp. 471–73 repr.
7   Published on Thursday 30 April 1778, p. 2.
8   Hayes 2001, p. 144.
9   These ideas were first expressed in a lecture by Duncan Robinson at Gainsborough's House, Sudbury, in about 1999.

10 *A Candid Review of the Exhibition*, London, May 1780, p. 19.

11 The source of the comment, quoted in W.T. Whitley, *Gainsborough*, London 1915, p. 170, is unknown.

12 In addition, a copy measuring 148 × 121.6 cm, lacking any of the subtlety of Gainsborough's handling, has recently come to light in New England. The provenance is as follows: Revd John Daubuz (1803/04–1883), London 1882; by descent to his son, John Claude Daubuz (1842–1914) by 1885; purchased by Thos. Agnew & Sons Ltd, in about 1898, reputedly for £6,000; purchased by Norman Forbes-Robertson (1858–1932) in 1903; his sale, Christie's, 19 May 1911, lot 105, bt Topham (£1050); purchased by Duveen Bros., New York; sold to Mrs B.F. Jones, Jr., Sewickley Heights, Penn (d. 1941); her posthumous sale, Parke-Bernet, New York, 4–5 December 1941, lot 12, bt "New York private collector" ($16,000); private collection; their anonymous sale, Parke-Bernet Galleries, New York, 22 September 1971, lot 125 (as School of Thomas Gainsborough), bt Benjamin A. Rifkin, New York ($1,600); acquired *c.* 2005 by Dr Elliot Sussman, Bethlehem, Pennsylvania. It was exhibited at the Royal Academy in 1882, no. 172; *Thomas Gainsborough*, Cincinnati Art Museum, May 1931, no. 24, pl. 19; Yale Center for British Art, New Haven, *c.* 2006 to January 2013. Sir Walter Armstrong included it in his monograph, *Gainsborough and His Place in British Art*, London 1898, p. 205 (1904 edition, p. 283). Benjamin A. Rifkin has recently produced an exhaustive study of the painting.

Another copy, measuring 152.4 × 121.9 cm, is known only from a reproduction (*Connoisseur*, CXLVI, October 1960, advertising supplement). It was in an anonymous sale, Town and Country Estates (Ireland) Ltd, Dublin, 9 November 1960 and subsequently with J.F.M. Leapman, London. John Hayes (1982, pp. 266, 480) lists other copies by Mrs Daniel Coppin (Norwich Castle Museum), showing the figure group, and one by John Crome (destroyed).

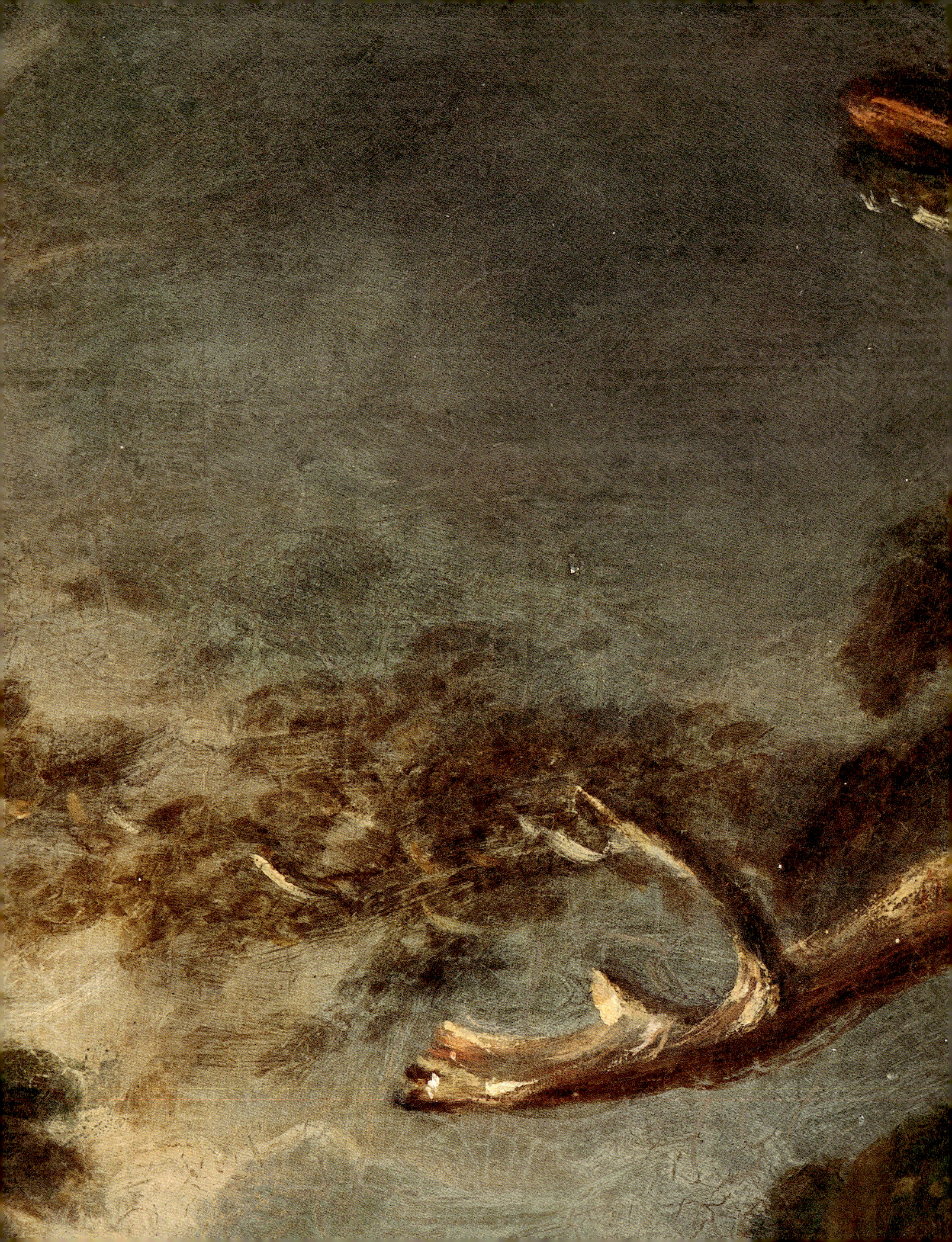

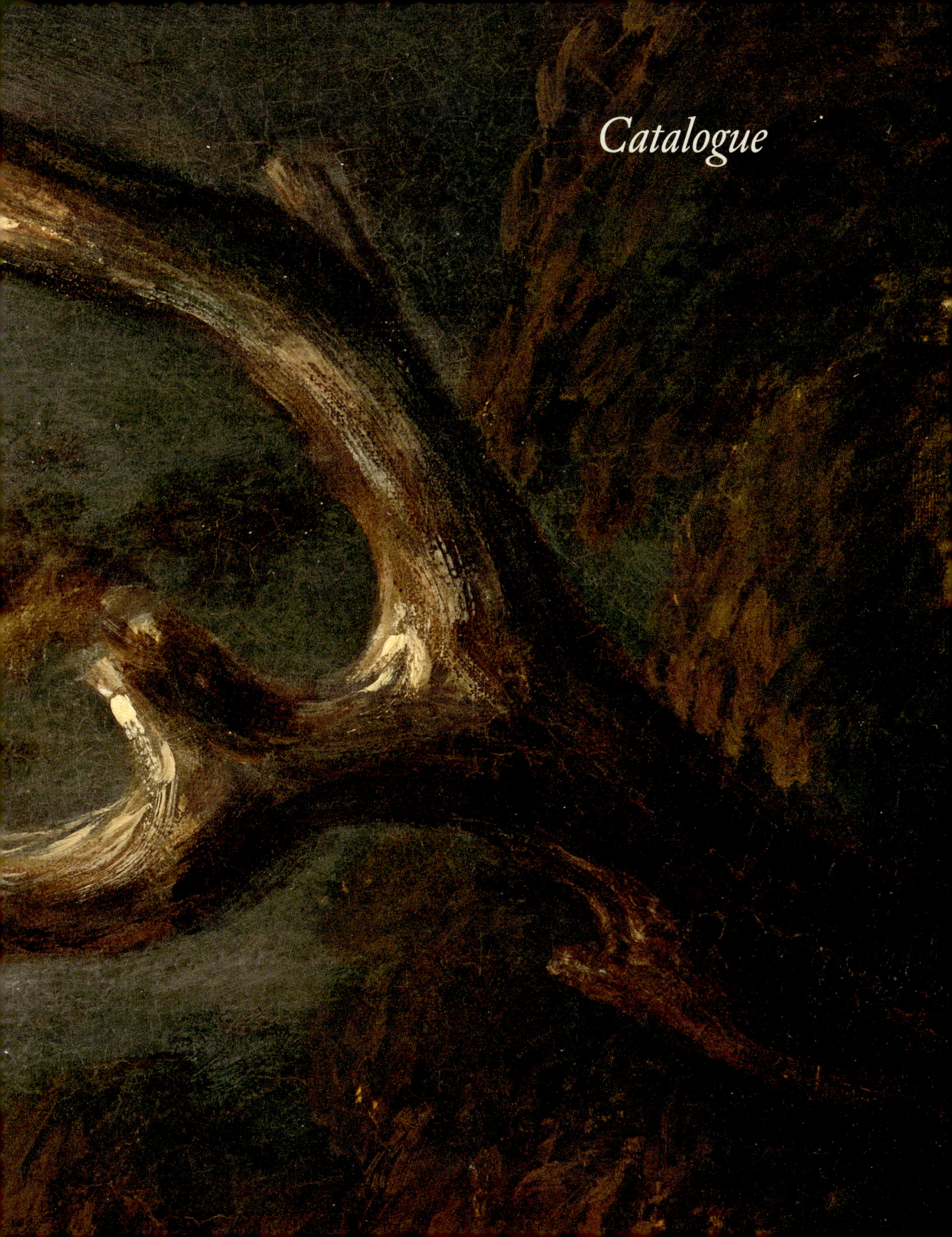
Catalogue

I   *The Cottage Door*, exhibited 1780

Oil on canvas, 147.3 × 119.4 cm
The Huntington Library, Art Collections, and Botanical Gardens,
San Marino

PROVENANCE Purchased in 1786 from the artist by Thomas Harvey (1748–1819), Catton House, Norfolk; perhaps with Mr Coppin; purchased by Sir John Leicester (1762–1827), later Lord de Tabley; his posthumous sale, Christie's, 7 July 1827, lot 52, bt Richard, 2nd Earl Grosvenor (1795–1869), later 2nd Marquess of Westminster; by descent to his great grandson, Hugh, 2nd Duke of Westminster (1879–1953); purchased by Duveen Bros; purchased by Henry E. Huntington (1850–1927), San Marino, California; bequeathed to the museum in 1927

EXHIBITIONS RA 1780 (no. 62); later exhibitions are listed by Asleson and Bennett 2001, p. 112

SELECTED LITERATURE listed by John Hayes, *The Landscapes of Thomas Gainsborough*, 2 vols., London 1982, pp. 477–78, and Robyn Asleson and Shelley M. Bennett, *British Paintings at the Huntington,* New Haven and London 2001, pp. 112–17; see also Ann Bermingham, *Sensation & Sensibility: Viewing Gainsborough's Cottage Door*, New Haven and London 2005, *passim*

See details on pp. 7, 98, 99, 101, 104

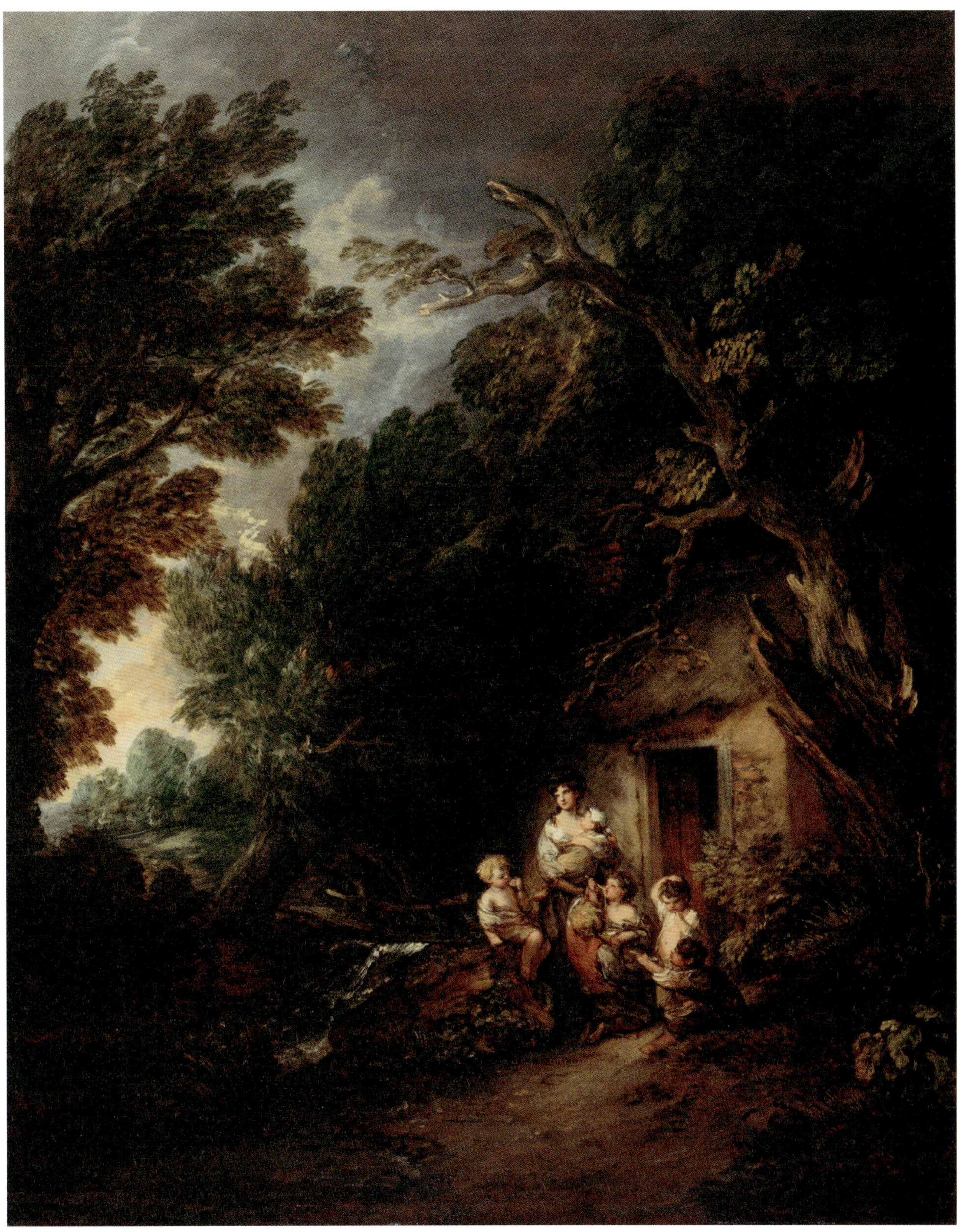

2   *The Cottage Door*, between 1780 and 1786

Oil on canvas, 148.2 × 120.4 cm
James Stunt

PROVENANCE The artist's posthumous sale, Schomberg House March
to May 1789, either no. 78 (*A landscape with a Cottage, Figures, &c*) or no.
69 (*A Landscape with a Cottage and Figures*); Wynne Ellis (1790–1875); his
posthumous sale, Christie's, 15 July 1876, lot 60, bt Partington (£100. 5s);
Ralph Cross Johnson; given to National Museum of Art, Smithsonian
Institution, USA; deaccessioned; Sotheby's New York, 4 June 1987, lot 135
[as 'After Thomas Gainsborough']; New Orleans Auction Galleries, 9–19
April 2011, lot 56 [as 'After Thomas Gainsborough'], bt Historical Portraits
Ltd, London; sold to the present owner in July 2012

EXHIBITIONS British Institution 1865, no. 161

SELECTED LITERATURE George B. Rose, 'The Ralph Cross Johnson
Collection at the National Gallery of Art', *Art and Archaelogy*, x, no. 3,
September 1920, pp. 342, 354 repr.; John Hayes, *The Landscapes of Thomas
Gainsborough*, 2 vols., London 1982, p. 480

See details on pp. 2, 66, 102, 103, 105, 107

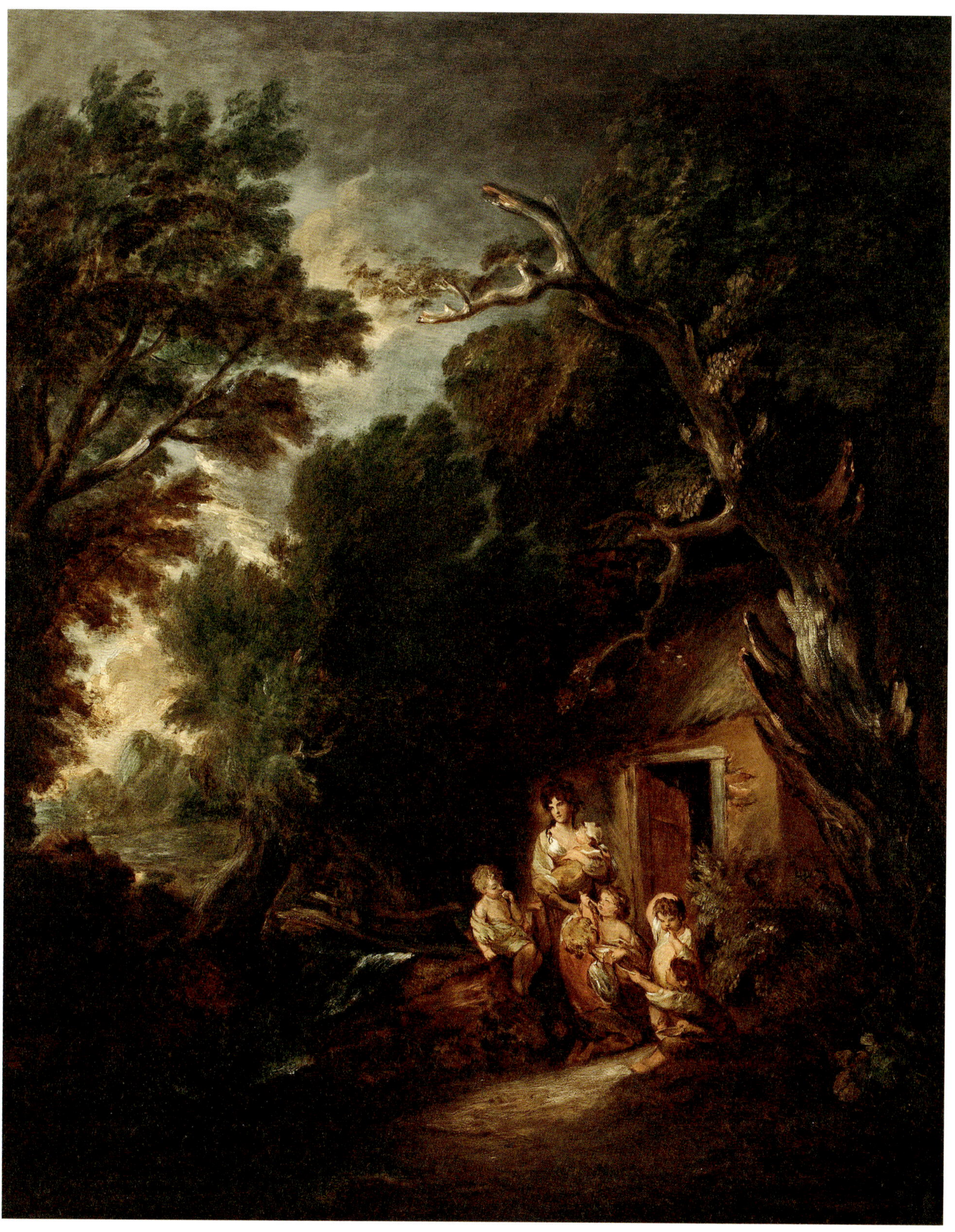

3   *The Cottage Door,* between 1780 and 1786

Oil on canvas, 149.8 × 121.3 cm
Private collection, Dallas

PROVENANCE The artist's posthumous sale, Schomberg House, March
to May 1789, either no. 78 (*A landscape with a Cottage, Figures, &c*) or
no. 69 (*A Landscape with a Cottage and Figures*); George Bowdler Gipps
(1853–1929), Canterbury; his sale, Christie's, 10 December 1910, lot 9;
private collection, Houston; Sotheby's, New York, 27 May 2004, lot 258,
repr. col., bt $21,600; with Historical Portraits, London; in January 2005
sold to a private collector, Dallas, through Deborah Gage Ltd; by descent

EXHIBITIONS *Sensation & Sensibility,* Yale Center for British Art, New
Haven; Huntington Library, San Marino 2005–06, unnumbered; *From
the Private Collections of Texas: European Art, Ancient to Modern*, Kimbell Art
Museum, Fort Worth, 22 November 2009 – 21 March 2010, pp. 226–27,
no. 45, repr. col.

SELECTED LITERATURE Ann Bermingham, *Sensation & Sensibility:
Viewing Gainsborough's Cottage Door*, New Haven and London 2005, pp. 3,
25–26, fig. 21 col.

See details on pp. 10, 111, 112

*Gainsborough's
Cottage Doors*

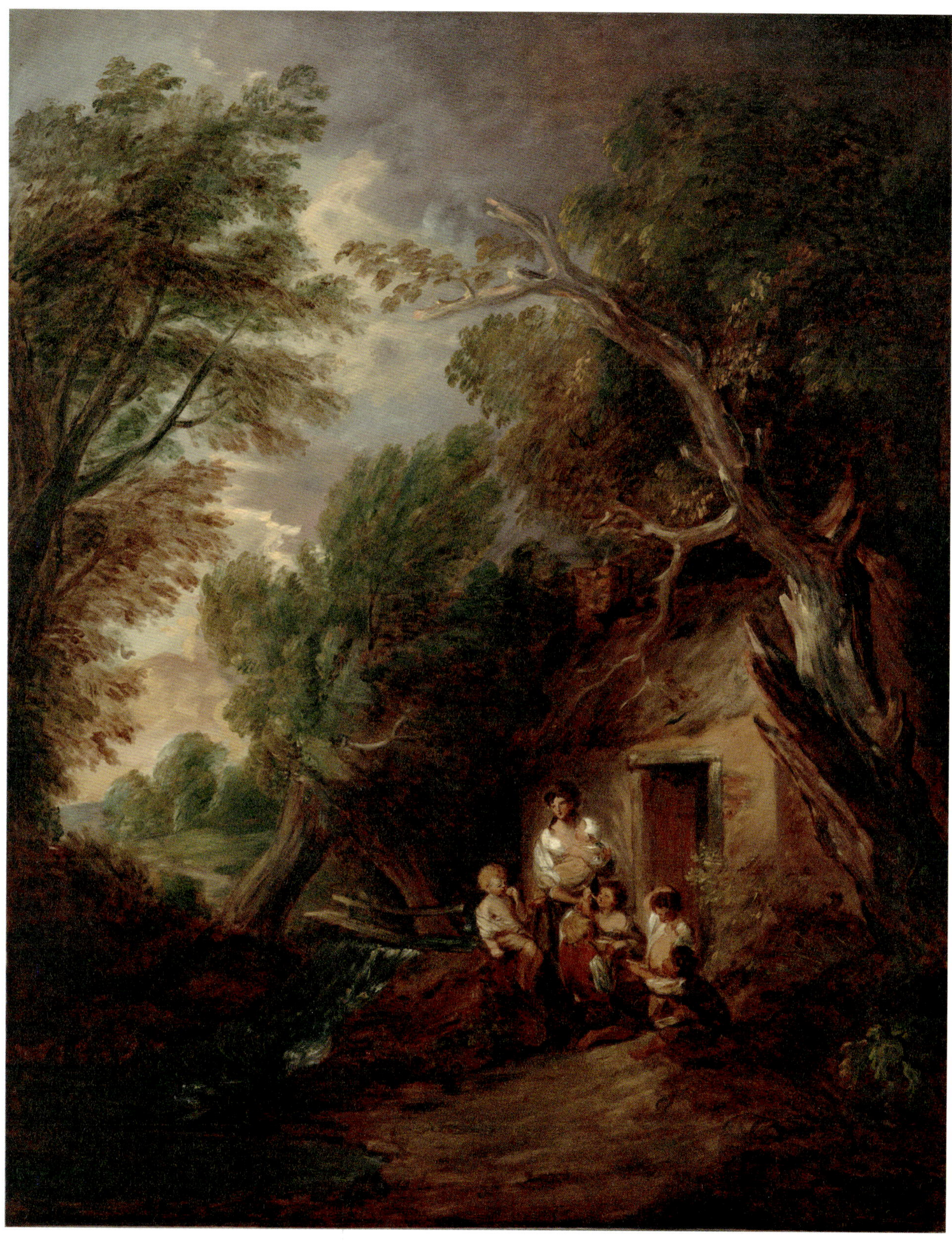

Cat. 1, figs. 20, 46, 47 © Courtesy of the Huntington Library, Art Collections, and Botanical Gardens, San Marino; cat. 2, fig. 48, 49 © James Stunt; cat. 3 © Private collection, Dallas; fig. 1 © Coram in the care of the Foundling Museum, London / The Bridgeman Art Library; fig. 2 Saint Louis Art Museum, Missouri, USA / The Bridgeman Art Library; fig. 3 National Gallery, London, UK / The Bridgeman Art Library; fig. 4 Private collection; fig. 5 © Holborne Museum, Bath; fig. 6 © National Portrait Gallery, London; figs, 7, 8 David Towersey; fig. 9 Private collection; fig. 10 from 'The Country Houses of Robert Adam', by Eileen Harris, published 2007 (b/w photo), English Photographer, (20th century) / © Country Life / The Bridgeman Art Library; fig. 11, 12, 22, 27, 44 The Royal Collection © 2013 HM Queen Elizabeth II; fig. 13, 15, 19, 24, 28, 33 © Trustees of the British Museum, London; fig. 14 © Scottish National Gallery, Edinburgh / The Bridgeman Art Library; fig. 16 © The Art Archive/Gulbenkian Foundation Lisbon/Gianni Dagli Orti; fig. 17 The National Gallery, London/akg-images; fig. 18 © Francis G. Mayer/Corbis; fig. 21 © Gainsborough's House, Sudbury; fig. 23, 29 © Royal Academy of Arts, London; fig. 25 Detroit Institute of Arts, USA / The Bridgeman Art Library; fig. 26 From the Castle Howard Collection. Reproduced with kind permission of the Hon. Simon Howard; fig. 30 Sterling & Francine Clark Art Institute, Williamstown, Massachusetts, USA / The Bridgeman Art Library; fig. 31 Private collection, London; fig. 32 © Newport Restoration Foundation, Rough Point, Newport; fig. 34 © National Gallery of Victoria, Melbourne; figs. 35, 36 © National Gallery of Art, Washington; fig. 37 © J. Paul Getty Museum, Los Angeles; fig. 38 Private collection, Los Angeles; fig. 39 © Chazen Museum of Art, Madison; fig. 40 © English Heritage Photo Library; fig. 41 Lowell Libson ltd; fig. 42 © Tokyo Fuji Art Museum, Tokyo, Japan / The Bridgeman Art Library; fig, 43 Cincinnati Art Museum, Ohio, USA / Given in honour of Mr & Mrs Charles F. Williams by their / children / The Bridgeman Art Library; fig. 45 Private collection; fig. 50 © Collection University of California, Los Angeles. Hammer Museum. The James Kennedy Collection. Photograph by the Getty Museum